LIVING WITH COLOUR

LIVING WITH COLOUR

The workbook
for managing
the colours
in your home

Deryck Healey

M

Macmillan
London

A Marshall Edition

Editor	Lewis Esson
Associate Editor	Shelley Turner
Editorial Assistants	Gwen Rigby
	Jazz Wilson
Art Editor	Simon Blacker
Design Assistant	Graeme Little
Picture Editor	Zilda Tandy
Production	Hugh Stancliffe

First published in 1982 by
Macmillan London Limited
London and Basingstoke

Associated companies in Auckland, Dallas, Delhi,
Dublin, Hong Kong, Johannesburg, Lagos, Manzini,
Melbourne, Nairobi, New York, Singapore, Tokyo,
Washington and Zaria

Living with Colour was conceived, edited and
designed by Marshall Editions Limited
71 Eccleston Square, London, SW1V 1PJ

ISBN 0 333 34176 7

Printed and bound in The Netherlands
by Smeets Royal Offset B.V., Weert

CONTENTS

FOREWORD

By Shirley Conran, author, journalist and designer

With colour, for the price of a pot of paint, people can express their own style and individuality. But, as with style, a gift for colour has to be developed by experiment. If you don't dare, you are doomed to dullness.

Most importantly, colour manipulates mood. An industrial colour consultant, like Deryck Healey, uses it to make an environment work; he might have to create an air of calm reassurance in a hospital, for instance, or a cheerful, stimulating atmosphere around a factory assembly-line. To sell a can or a car, the designer will attract a customer, stimulate interest, make a product look cheap or expensive or different from its competitors – mainly using colour.

Nobody is born with a fully developed colour sense or a perfect colour memory and you *can't* learn how to use colour from books of theory, they can only explain what you have already discovered from your own experience.

You have to discover and develop your *own* colour style, just as a child learns creative play with building bricks; and the process should be as easy and enjoyable as childs' play. Anyone who has been to art school will probably have developed an experimental attitude to colour, without thinking much about it. He or she is likely to look upon colour trial in the home as a store window-dresser does: sticking bits of tissue, fabric or coloured paper against a wall; pinning a towel on a window frame and seeing not the towel, but the finished curtain hanging there.

Most people first use colour to express their personalities when selecting and combining their clothes, and they usually get most daring when they are buying a bright shirt to wear on the beach, as opposed to one in which to visit the bank manager. This is the happy, expectant attitude to colour that should also prevail in your home, where you can also be completely yourself and not worry about your public image.

The development of your own colour sense takes time; you learn that what works in theory often doesn't work in practice, because theory is based on a perfect situation and life ain't like that.

The easiest way to learn to use colour (as with everything) is to work with someone who is good at it and has had a lot of experience – like Deryck Healey. To stay in his country house is to be in the most delightful atmosphere of colour experiment; something is always going on, being pinned up or tried out, either in his messy studio, his immaculate drawing room, in a corner of his ancient rectory garden or his gleaming modern kitchen. The never-ending fascination and exhilaration that you see in Deryck's home and work is what he manages to convey so well. It has already given me great pleasure and will continue to do so. I hope that you will also find that, like colour itself, this book is an investment in pleasure.

Shirley Conran

Pierre Bonnard *Le Déjeuner*

INTRODUCTION

Pierre Bonnard lived and breathed colour. His paintings radiate both a love and an understanding of the richest medium to meet our senses. In depicting normal, everyday interior scenes, he transposed their cosy reality into his own favourite mauves, lilacs, oranges, pinks, violet-blues and yellows, to produce an effect that is simultaneously vibrant and serene.

He and his fellow Impressionist painters shared the excitement of using a new colour palette of unabashedly pure, strong hues, combined in magical proportions. With it, they joyously illuminated quite ordinary subject matter, and such works allow us to perceive colour through the eyes of professionals devoted to exploring its many aspects. Their vision makes the heart leap with effortless delight and there is no reason why the colours in your own home should not do the same.

Living with Colour is a guide to the discovery and development of your personal colour sense. With it, you can make your relationship to colour active rather than passive – much like the difference between listening appreciatively to a piece of music, instead of just overhearing it. You can learn how colour is not just a sensation – even a pleasurable sensation – but a means of highly individual expression.

In the same way that an artist is described as having a 'palette' – the particular colours with which he or she is identified – we tend, as we go through life, to evolve our own spontaneous palettes, reflected in clothes, cosmetics and possessions, as well as decorating. *Living with Colour* suggests ways in which to make this palette less random, arbitrary or timid, so that you can squeeze out of colour more of the goodness that it has to offer.

Today's world teems with unprecedented quantities of colour stimuli. At the touch of a television dial, we are transported from the shimmering metallics of a space-shuttle launch to the lush red-carpeted interiors of *Gone with the Wind*, to the irridescent splendours of a documentary on exotic tropical wildlife. Such broad exposure is nowadays taken for granted as part of our daily diet of colour, and it is backed up by the infinite range of paints, papers, fabrics, tiles, floor coverings and other decorating materials available to us. However, it is only when you begin to choose and use colour for your own needs that its power has real impact on your lifestyle.

Living with Colour opens your eyes to the perspectives of other eras, the attitudes of foreign cultures and the demands of many different disciplines. It shows how the things you already own – whether an important carpet or sofa, a favourite painting or a collection of seashells – can set a striking, original scheme in motion. It gives you a peep at the private use of colour by those for whom it is a way of life – from Monet's dining-room to Zandra Rhodes's bedroom. Let them help liberate your notions of what is suitable where; any colour you love can go in any room you like.

Home decorating must satisfy needs which are personal, practical and social; colour accomodates all three. In devising schemes, Art and Nature offer limitless inspiration – whether a turn around the Tate Gallery or a walk in autumn woods. *Living with Colour* aims to make the vital connection between the beauty you respond to in the outside world and the realities of paints and patterns. I hope that it will give you the confidence to be newly creative, so that from now on you will feel truly at home with colour.

DH 1982

To my mother, who encouraged my involvement in home decorating from when I was first able to hold a paintbrush, and to my sister.

Inspirations from the past

Our understanding of the science of colour and today's advanced technology of dye and pigment manufacture have us awash with a range of colours almost as rich as that produced by Nature herself. We are so spoiled for choice that we are in danger of taking too much for granted, becoming jaded and ceasing to see and enjoy the chromatic richness we now possess.

To our ancestors, the chemistry of colour was akin to that of alchemy – it really was magic. Certain colours were made from materials so rare that they were the preserve of the ruling élite or the priestly classes.

Somehow such constraints never seemed to cramp the style of early artists and decorators. In fact, the opposite was often the case. The rarity value gave artisans a true sense of the power of colour, and the result was consummate skill and visible joy in its use; their expertise and enthusiasm can be an inspiration to us still.

The electric primary colours of Egypt; the cool marble hues of the Ancient Greeks; the rich warm tones of Imperial Rome; the subtle shades of the Orient and the gem-like glitter of Arabia have all been influences on past generations. As empires waxed, and old glories, such as that of Egypt, were either brought back by conquering soldiers or painstakingly dug up by archaeologists, successive generations have been given fresh stimulus. They interpreted such colour usage in a myriad different ways, creating their own distinctive styles, from which we can also learn.

Today our abundance of colour choice is matched by the easy access we have to the evocative riches of the past. Whether it be in the wealth of our local museums, the lavish illustrations on our library shelves, or even the exaggerated sumptuousness of epic movie sets, we are surrounded by mankind's colourful history.

The Empress Josephine's extravagantly romantic bedroom in her Château de la Malmaison reflects the influence both of Napoleon's conquest of Egypt and the discoveries at Pompeii.

THE VALLEY OF THE NILE

The breath-taking works of Ancient Egypt are lasting evidence of the source to which most Western art and architecture may be traced.

Unique features of Egyptian culture made its influence more than merely seminal. The Egyptians made their artefacts from only the most precious, and least corruptible, materials and hid them away in sealed tombs so that their full glory was unfaded when subsequent generations uncovered them.

The Egyptians strove to create fine reproductions of themselves and their surroundings that they might be afforded the immortality denied the flesh. In so doing they left an extraordinarily sharp image of their world, one that has given fresh inspiration directly to many cultures and generations.

The Egyptians took their own inspiration from their surroundings. The intensity of the desert sun and the fertility of the Nile valley are reflected in the colours of Egyptian decorative art.

The Victorian romantics were excited and inspired by Owen Jones's *Grammar of Ornament* published in 1856. This page displayed to great effect the Ancient Egyptian decoration then to be seen, particularly in the Cairo Museum.

Jones certainly shows the strength of the influence of Nature on Egyptian decoration. The geometry of petal and leaf formations has echoes in the motif on Tutankhamun's cloak.

Even the zig-zag pattern of the water is coloured with tints of green, red, white and black. This reflects the cycle that the Egyptians saw in the annual flood of the Nile, which stirred up mud and

The Egyptians believed that the soul would live on only if the body were preserved; and, where that was impossible, they made replicas of the body. Tutankhamun's body was mummified and then encased in two sarcophagi which were both elaborately carved and decorated to depict him in full regal splendour. In this way not only was he provided with

multiple indemnity, but he was assured that his shroud windings would not force him to go unrecognized as a great king in the afterworld.

The coffin decoration shows the king dressed for a state occasion. The lapis lazuli and precious gems embedded in the solid gold of this, the outer coffin, might well have decorated delicate gold garments worn by the living king.

mineral deposits and coloured the water strongly.

The central image is a representation of lotus and papyrus stalks, bound with coloured matting and ribbons to form a column with an elaborate capital – mimicked on stone pillars.

Today the Egyptian influence is interpreted in many ways. This starkly dramatic interior in the home of a leading Italian couturier evokes a desert landscape flooded with bright morning light. A pyramid is framed by two plain Egyptian columns and, in turn, by two palm trees, which appear black in silhouette.

A more intimate, but equally theatrical, effect has been given to this modern Parisian bedroom by meticulously recreating the interior of an Egyptian royal tent – rich in pattern on pattern.

Owen Jones's influential book was reprinted in 1911 and provided fresh stimulus to twentieth-century designers. Then, in 1922, the tomb of Tutankhamun was discovered. It was the only undisturbed Pharonic tomb to be opened in modern times and the sheer material value of its contents captured even the most unaesthetic imagination, while the rich decoration stimulated the new generation of artists and architects involved in creating the Art Deco style of the 1920s and '30s.

Behind the 'Odeon'-style façades and the ziggurat stepping of new tall buildings were attempts to recreate the interior glories of the richly inlayed, polished gold surfaces in the tombs themselves.

This 1930s bathroom made bold use of strongly reflective gold wall tiles; the patterning is reminiscent of that on Tutankhamun's coffin. The softly varying green glazes on the floor tiles, and the stepped ceiling, further enhance the Egyptian effect. The bright whites, both reflective and matt, of the bathroom fittings, the engraved glass and the concealed neon lighting heighten the drama of the interior, while preventing it from looking overly tomb-like.

CLASSICAL GREECE

The Ancient Greeks were, above all, masters of proportion and geometry. Theirs was a culture whose artists were unfettered by the need to honour their gods with symbolic decoration; they concentrated on celebrating life, rather than depicting the afterlife, and practised art for art's sake. The result was a perfection of form that has served as a model ever since.

As their society developed, they were much influenced by the Egyptians and they painted their great stone temples every bit as gaudily as those in the valley of the Nile. Unfortunately, that original coloration was worn away by the elements and possibly even removed by later generations, and by the Romans, who regarded the painting of buildings as vulgar and degenerate. But their highly-coloured and geometrically patterned marble walls and tiled floors have survived to provide a continuing influence.

There have been many revivals of 'classical' style, usually accompanied by an attempt to restore the humanistic values of the ancients' 'age of reason' as exemplified in the grace and proportions of their art and architecture. The works of the sixteenth-century Italian architect, Palladio, were probably among the most influential. A wave of romanticism which swept across Europe in the early eighteenth century renewed interest in his work and began the first wholly consistent revival we now term Neo-classicism.

In England and France the Palladian revival was further fuelled by the publication in the mid-eighteenth century of richly illustrated works on the recently ruined Parthenon. This was known as the 'Greek revival' phase of the movement, and its major proponent was Robert Adam. Many of his interiors exemplified the 'noble simplicity' and 'calm grandeur' that were held to be the virtues of Ancient Greece and their manner of decoration.

Apart from stonework, and faded patches on wall friezes and pieces of sculpture, the only real examples of Greek colour ornament to survive were in the form of painted pottery. Vases (amphorae) and cups (*kylices*), were decorated inside and out. The familiar black silhouette figures on a ground of red clay, and later red figures etched out of the black paint, reinforced the belief that the Greeks had consciously avoided the use of bright colours. This left a lasting impression of classic Greek colour usage as being deliberately restrained.

This entrance hall to Osterley Park, near London, which Robert Adam designed for Robert Child in 1773, impressively exhibits the elements of his 'Greek revival' style.

They include a granite-grey, geometric, marbled floor; draped, bas-relief figures and statuary, and white, fretted key-pattern moulding which runs as a cornice along the tops of the walls. The ceiling is seemingly supported by *trompe-l'œil* pillars.

The pale blue used on the walls and ceiling was probably chosen by Adam from then currently fashionable colours inspired by imported Chinese porcelain glazes.

Such cool blues and greens provided the most flattering setting for the furniture characteristic of the period, as the contrast with the rich, dark wood doors demonstrates.

Classical gusto is exhibited by a group of Italian fabric, wallpaper, ceramic and furniture designers who have collaborated to produce a stylized update of Greek design in suitably cool colours.

A Mediterranean-blue hallway is adorned with an amphora-motif paper and a similar image, used large-scale, framed by a key-pattern border. The mural is also reflected in the stool upholstery.

The earthy tones used in this bathroom are reminiscent of the red clay of amphorae. The similarity is also evident in the clever use of counterchanged light motifs on dark grounds and vice versa – a direct parallel to that of the Ancient Greek black- and red-figuring.

The effect enriches the overall patterning and gives the impression that there are many more colours at work.

This wallpaper frieze by Walter Crane he christened 'Alcestis' after a queen of Thessaly who gave her life in place of that of her husband. Caryatids (female figure columns) represent the virtues of Diligence, Order, Providence and Hospitality.

At the Philadelphia Exhibition of 1876 the paper was awarded a medal for 'great excellence and chastity of design . . . with exceedingly harmonious colouring.' The manufacturers were also commended for 'works of art in paper decoration which . . . tend to elevate paper as a decorative article.'

This celebration of the ancient virtues helped to establish wallpapers as 'socially acceptable.'

IMPERIAL ROME

The Romans literally turned architecture 'outside-in'. Renowned as great engineers, theirs was the first society to take advantage of the economy and practicality of concrete: mortar and gravel, mixed with rubble. Using its strength and flexibility they built on an heroic scale that, for the first time, put the emphasis on the space inside buildings and not on cosmetic façades or the celebration of pillars and supports.

This was reflected in their domestic architecture. The well-to-do Romans built homes that were windowless to the outside world, taking their light instead from internal courtyards, or atriums, in search of privacy and seclusion in an increasingly commercial urban society.

Not surprisingly, the interiors of these villas were lavishly decorated in brilliant colours. Walls were elaborately painted to mimic marble or were covered with murals. The Romans were the first to explore fully the possibilities of *trompe-l'œil* painting on walls, in an attempt to depict gardens or fabulous landscapes beyond their confines. Fortunately, for us at least, much of this was preserved for posterity when the towns of Pompeii and Herculaneum were buried in AD79 by an eruption of the volcano, Mount Vesuvius.

The Roman Empire was truly 'international'. Its geographic extent was such that it left its mark in places as far apart as Asia Minor and England. It also absorbed and accommodated aspects of its vassal cultures that it liked or found it convenient to adopt.

Foremost of these was the Greek influence, which was so strong that Roman art is often said to have been merely the last, decadent, stage of Greek art. Until the uncovering of more evidence at sites like Pompeii, this must have been all too easy to believe. Roman buildings, whatever their grandeur, had been made only of concrete and then clad in plaster, brick or veneers of marble, all of which were eroded by time – leaving mighty ruins that, although awesome in scale, looked shabby and second-rate compared to their Greek antecedents.

The Roman prefects and merchants, however, built their villas in distant marches of the Empire using the eclectic styles that they had observed as fashionable in 'The City'. Such rich colour use, based on Etruscan, Egyptian, Greek and Persian art, and the Roman love of life and Nature, was thus transfused throughout most of Europe.

The House of the Vetti family was one of the many exciting finds made in the eighteenth century, when the cities of Pompeii and Herculaneum were excavated from their mummifying layers of volcanic debris. The wall paintings, although featuring panels depicting myths of many cultures in a distinctly Greek style, exhibit a fresh, Roman approach to perspective in the *trompe-l'œil* windows.

In the spectacular Glass Drawing Room Robert Adam created in 1775, for the wealthy Duke of Northumberland, every bit of wall is either mirrored or panelled with red glass. The mysterious depth and myriad perspectives created by such a design, together with the elaborate gilt decoration, seem a clear reflection of the recent archaeological discoveries like the room above.

In the Middle Ages, wall paintings gave way to richly worked tapestries. Important warming elements in drear Gothic citadels, they preserved the theme of outdoor vistas.

In Renaissance palaces, like the fourteenth-century Palazzo Davanzati in Florence, the wall-illusion process went full circle. Elaborately gilded and painted designs attempted to emulate rich Gothic tapestry hangings.

William Morris's wallpaper embodies his pioneering design philosophy of 'made by the people, and for the people, as a happiness to the maker and the user'. In the late nineteenth century, he strove to displace the bankrupt and increasingly debased over-ornamentation of Neoclassicism by creating a new style, 'The Arts and Crafts Movement', with a similarly Romantic basis – the Gothic.

Mariano Fortuny spent his formative years, at the turn of the century, in Rome and his mother's palazzo, on the Grand Canal in Venice. The rich early stimulus of such surroundings was reflected in his exquisite hand-blocked and overpainted fabrics, and in dress designs that were revolutionary in both the technical and social sense. His works, described by his celebrated contemporary, the novelist Marcel Proust, as 'faithfully antique, but markedly original,' have proved to be a continuing influence on most twentieth-century fashion, textile and interior designers.

TURNING TO THE EAST

The Spice Trade with the East has existed since the beginning of recorded history. The same merchants who brought condiments to revive bored Athenian palates also brought examples of Oriental art and artefacts, which similarly stimulated the jaded tastes of successive generations.

Europeans were fascinated by the totally alien style they exhibited and intrigued by the skills and technology obviously required to produce such fine work. Chinese wallpaper, lacquered screens and inlaid boxes were all closely examined and attempts made to copy them, with varying degrees of success.

One science, however, remained totally elusive, that of the manufacture of porcelain. As early as the ninth century, a traveller had reported, 'They have

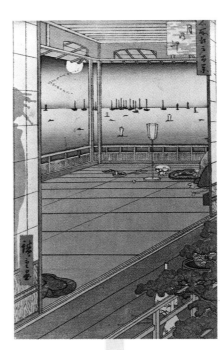

During the Sung dynasty, AD 960-1279, the Chinese brought their art of porcelain manufacture to perfection. This was also the period when its products became known abroad. A trade in 'céladon ware' developed, particularly in the Islamic states, when in AD 1171, Saladin – greatly taken by the hypnotic depth and softness of the cool blues and yellowish greens of the glazes – made a gift of forty pieces of it to the Sultan of Damascus.

in China a very fine clay with which they make vases, which are as transparent as glass; water is seen through them.' It was not simply the exquisite translucence that bewitched, but the unique and enchanting colours of its glazing. It is probably no accident that where we use the terms 'light' and 'dark' to describe the intensity of a colour, the Chinese employ 'shallow' and 'deep'.

It was not until 1708 that a young German alchemist stumbled across the secret of high-temperature firing of clay, using the oxides of various metals to produce a wide range of glaze colours. This discovery gave rise to the Meissen factories, and within a few decades porcelain manufacture had spread to Sèvres in France and to the Wedgwood potteries in England – in time to catch the European vogue for *chinoiserie*.

As European traders were establishing routes throughout the Far East, the repressive military dictators of Japan, the *shogun,* closed the country off to all foreigners. It remained an enigma to the West until the mid-eighteenth century, when the Meiji Restoration overthrew the shogunate and sent missions abroad. Colourful wood-blocks in harmonious flat, matt tones, like Andó Hiroshige's *Interior of a Tea House with a View of the Sea* executed circa 1840, were to be a great influence on Western artists and architects.

The interior of the imposing family seat of the princes of Udaipur exhibits the painting, wood-carving and intricate and highly coloured inlay work for which the Indian sub-continent has long been celebrated. In the sixteenth century, Islamic warriors gained hegemony over the Hindu princes to establish the glittering Moghul Empire. Its seeming sudden splendour, exhibited in wonders like the Taj Mahal, attracted the jackdaw eyes of Europe's merchant adventurers.

In the seventeenth century, the tile makers of Delft in Holland took their inspiration from Ming dynasty (AD1368-1644) blue-and-white porcelain and were instrumental in making this a signal element in the later craze for 'The Chinese Taste'. Louis XIV's original Trianon, built in 1670, was entirely covered in such tiles and was widely copied. The kitchen of the Amalienburg hunting lodge in the park of Nymphenburg Castle, home of the Bavarian royal family, is a fine example of such influence.

The Royal Pavilion in Brighton nicely demonstrates the confusion of India and China suffered by most of the eighteenth-century English. Its gilded 'onion' domes make it one of the world's best-known follies, while the interior is in a lavish Chinese style. Built by the Prince of Wales in the 1780's to house his morganatic wife Mrs Fitzherbert, he returned to it after an enforced state marriage to Princess Caroline of Brunswick and celebrated reunion with his true love in a frenzy of romantic redecoration.

Thomas Chippendale was one of the first furniture manufacturers to realize the possibilities offered by 'The Chinese Taste'. He produced chairs like this one, which is even red-lacquered and embellished with gilt ornament using pagoda motifs. More restrained designs often had the square leg, the latticework back and carving, imitating bamboo. His fame spread widely after the publication, in 1754, of his *Gentleman and Cabinet-maker's Director*.

Today the Oriental influence is interpreted in many ways. The use of gilt-inlaid black-lacquered furniture and a richly patterned print on the walls and the upholstery gives a modern version of romantic *chinoiserie*. A more subtle effect is obvious in the trend towards the 'minimal', instilling tranquillity by the use of spare interiors containing only one or two fine items to inspire meditation.

LOOKING TO MECCA

The sudden rise of Islam, in the century after Muhammad's death in AD 632, created an empire stretching from the Pyrenees to north-west China, synthesizing the waning cultures of the Mediterranean and Near East, and forging a bridge between Orient and Occident.

Much of Islam's initial artistic and architectural influence was derived from the Greco-Roman heritage of Byzantium. This was most evident in the enthusiastic decoration of all surfaces, interior and exterior, with mosaic and, later, glazed tiling.

Muhammad had condemned idolatry and, from about the eighth century, this was interpreted as a stricture against the representation of human or animal forms. Hence calligraphy and stylized floral and abstract geometric decoration became the prime constituents of Muslim art. As a result, a love of brilliant colours also became characteristic.

It was the conquest of Spain in AD 700 that brought the life and vigour of Islamic art and learning to medieval Europe. The joyful play of arches in the Great Mosque of Córdoba and the fairy-tale tracery of the vaulting in the Alhambra Palace at Granada left an indelible mark on the West.

Chinese influence was infused into the Persian corner of the Islamic empire by the invasion of the Mongols in the thirteenth century. From this developed the rich tradition of Persian miniatures, illuminated manuscripts, and textile, rug and ceramic work.

It was to suit the taste of these Persians that the Chinese began to produce blue-and-white painted porcelain which was eventually not only to become popular in China itself, but to spark off the fashion for blue-and-white stoneware and tiling all over the civilized world.

The Ottoman Turks kept Islamic influence thriving in Europe from the conquest of Constantinople in 1453 until the end of the First World War.

Both eighteenth-century and Victorian romantics found the Arab world a source of fascination – the more so when *The Thousand and One Nights* was translated and popularized. This, in turn, inspired the Ballets Russes production of *Schéhérézade* which left its glittering mark on Edwardian fashion and furnishing. Even now, Arab imagery – magic lamps and flying carpets, shimmering domes and palms, billowing tents and veils – remains the essence of fantasy.

The Masjid-i-Shah, or Imperial Mosque, in Isfahan, built by Shah Abbas I in the early seventeenth century, is one of the later and finest flowerings of Islamic building and decoration. The rich turquoise tile glaze is predominant, studded with a deep cobalt blue and greens, browns and purples.

The Marquis of Aragon had this villa built for him in Tuscany in 1605. The royal House of Aragon had been instrumental in driving the Moors out of Spanish territory. This vivid, High-Renaissance interpretation of Arab style has something of the Baroque, then just developing in Rome.

A modern interior in North Africa demonstrates a more restrained approach to the traditional elements. Solid yellow walls are bound by tiling and painted stucco in more muted colours.

Reaction against the drab uniformity of the machine age led the Victorians into a fresh phase of romanticism. The rich preferred neoclassic; while aesthetes like Lord Leighton, a celebrated artist of his time, turned again to the east. The Arab Hall at Leighton House in London used antique Syrian tiles and carved shutters.

Léon Bakst's sets and costumes for the Ballets Russes dazzled the Parisians with the most exuberant range of colours and patterns ever seen on stage. Sets like that for *Les Orientales*, in 1910, put the tile-glaze tones of mustard, cobalt blue and turquoise into every fashionable home.

INSPIRATIONS FROM AROUND THE WORLD

As the jet age shrinks the world for us, our visual horizons expand. We are now in the enviable position of being able to travel with ease anywhere over the rainbow, and of having the world's wealth of design brought to us via travelling exhibitions.

Only miles from some of the world's busiest airports, decked out in the best of 'international style', there are still tribes using stone-age implements and pigments to decorate their dwellings. As our understanding and use of colour develops, we have not lost contact with its spiritual beginnings.

Even the armchair traveller can benefit from the stimulus of exposure to other cultures, gloriously illustrated by books, magazine articles and the mass media, bouncing live pictures from one side of the globe to the other.

Differences of climate, geography and related skin colour have endowed the planet's various races with a pleasurable diversity in their perception and manipulation of colour. Their multifarious frames of reference have long been a rich source of stimulus for the decorator. The warm floral gaiety of Europe's folk art; the earthy magic of Africa; the sophisticated intensity of the Indian sub-continent; the natural harmonies of the Amerindians; the joyous primaries of Latin America, or the studied neutrality of Japan – can all be imported into your interior schemes.

Whether a striking postcard merely brings the exotic to your doorstep or travel actually takes you to far-off places, seize any opportunity you can to learn a new colour language.

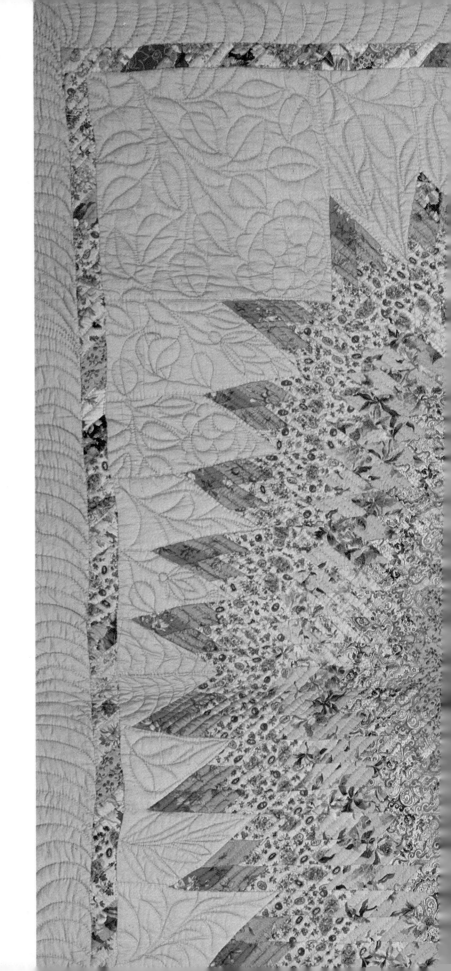

A turn-of-the-century American patchwork quilt radiates the charm and energy of folk art; its soft, morning-light coloration, befitting the sunburst motif, appropriately symbolic of the dawning of a new culture.

EUROPEAN FOLK ART

The late glories of Europe's cultural Renaissance in the sixteenth century were the preserve of the courtly nobility and urban middle classes. The broad mass of Europe's peasantry made do with a culture of its own, passed on, by example, from one generation to the next. It was based on highly practical demands, employing a symbolism and colour use that was of great ritual significance: for instance, during the fertility rite celebrations of spring and the giving of thanks for the harvest in the autumn.

Considering how narrow the limits of experience of such folk must have been, there is astonishing similarity in the products of their art from widely separated corners of the continent. What seems to unite them is their sheer love of Nature's visual beauty and their joyfully innocent use of bright colours to adorn both themselves and their surroundings.

It has been suggested that this natural delight in decorative colour and form can be traced to an earlier primordial culture. This might explain the fact that various regions like the Kurpie district in Poland and Appenzell in Switzerland, for example, have such a similarly spirited tradition. Certainly, many of the Eastern European communities have also inherited some distinct traits reflecting incursions by the Ottoman Turks and earlier Mongol invaders.

It is much more likely that the art of the folk of Europe arose from similar needs to celebrate the very natural forces which gave them their livelihood, and was modified by the raw materials at their disposal in each area.

Colour use certainly does seem to vary widely from area to area. The Romanians, for instance, put little colour on the outside of their buildings, while their Hungarian neighbours decorate theirs with vigour. These differences may be cultural or practical, depending simply on climate or availability of pigment.

The many rich traditions and skills from all over Europe were invaluable when the New World was settled, mostly by the poorer classes in search of a new life. Peoples from different countries set up communities in various parts of North America, and the pioneering conditions led to a fresh flourishing of their own native arts and crafts: a 'rural renaissance' which was eventually to give birth to a new and distinctive American style.

Hungarian embroidery, satin-stitched on linen, using stylized floral motifs, is the domestic version of the vivid polychrome embroidery employed by their tailors to embellish garments for both men and women. Young girls create delicately worked colourful table-cloths and bed-covers as part of their dowry. Shirts, blouses, bodices and shawls are all richly embroidered; as are male outer garments. These are decorated according to the wearer's social standing in the community.

A farmer in the Zalipie district of Poland stands proudly by his horse in a stable that has been gaily decorated, freehand, with bunches of large lush flower motifs in blue, red and black on a white ground.

It is not surprising that particular decorative attention is lavished on the everyday items of country folks' working lives: their carved crooks, staffs, whip-butts and drinking vessels. As with every farmer, the horse is this man's most prized possession and valuable asset. The stable door has been decked out like a picture frame, the better to set off the features of the noble beast.

Weavers in various districts in the Highlands of medieval Scotland took to giving their woollen fabrics distinctive bands of colours. The extraordinarily tight Picto-Celtic tribal system flourished into a type of feudalism particular to the Scots, as during the fifteenth and sixteenth centuries the feudal system seem to die away in the rest of Europe. The system of clans, from *clanna* meaning children, was an elaborate patriarchy with no peasant class and a non-caste aristocracy.

The close ties each clan held with its tribal lands led the tartans made by the weavers of each district to be adopted as tribal costume.

As families intermingled and moved to different areas, the tartans became increasingly complex – the background colours of one being shot through with a couple of lines of each of the colours of another – developing ultimately into one of the world's most unusually simple, but effective and highly decorative systems of heraldry.

The thatched Polish cottage is brightly painted in the two colours most likely to contrast vividly with the green of the surrounding countryside – blue and red. Such bold use of primary colours is echoed in the national costume. From the picking-out of the carved mouldings on the shutters and doors of such buildings developed a particularly Polish craft of bedecking the walls of houses with pieces of coloured paper, cut, while folded, to give silhouettes of stars and flowers. In some districts, more paper shapes in contrasting colours are pasted over these to give even more impressive effects.

AFRICA

The 'Dark Continent' is deceptively filled with subtle colour and wreathed with its magic.

A simple life, based on Nature's favours, has given the native tribes of Africa a serene bond with the rich diversity of the land. Some, like the N'Debele of the south, may paint the walls of their houses and their *kraals* with bright colours; while others, like the Massa of the Cameroon, make the domed huts that moved writer André Gide to talk of 'a beauty so perfect, so accomplished, that it seems natural. No ornament, no superfluity. . .' But they all make use of mud, so enshrining both the strength and the colour of the earth in their homes. The clay walls, sometimes smoothed by washing and scouring until they gleam like mirrors, vary in hue from the lightest of greys to a rich deep red. The furnishings and utensils: reed bed-mats, calabash gourds, straw baskets and clay pots, all remain in keeping with this terrene coloration.

Fresh blue and white are commonly used in interiors and on clothing and bedding, and green occasionally appears as an external wall embellishment – all the common colours of the wide-open spaces. In recognition of its power, more vivid colour is reserved for ritual decoration and communication: the painting of bodies at times of war and festivity, or the accentuation of the features on masks and fetishes for fertility and initiation rites.

A Nigerian poet most succinctly told the colour story of his continent when, celebrating his homeland, he talked of his wish to 'answer her communal call, /Lose myself in her warm caress/ Intervolving earth, sky and flesh.'

Blue and white patterns are popular throughout Africa, in a wide variety of stripes and checks. The colouring matter is probably indigo, extracted from plants – one of man's oldest dyestuffs. It is used to give a variety of hues from deep navy and sky-blue to a light slate. Its effect is cool and refreshing in such unremittingly neutral surroundings.

The parents' bed-mat is probably a prized wedding gift, and is decorated with thick ochre bands and a scattering of ochre and deep brown stencilled flowers.

The Masai tribe of East Africa have been particularly resistent to cultural change throughout the centuries. Renowned as warriors, they are actually a pastoral people more intent on guarding their precious cattle. Their nomadic existence has compelled them to concentrate their decorative skills on the body and on dress, and a craft of elaborate beadwork has evolved, which incorporates a complex colour and design communication code. Such neckwear may well be made up of cherished love letters, assertions of virginity or even statements of family wealth and, thus, dowry potential.

A typical courtyard in Mauritania, shows the use of whitewash as both an interior coating for cleanliness and coolness and as ornament on the red clay walls. Windows and doors are frequently banded with white to fend off evil spirits. The whitewash would normally be made from a solution of a chalky clay. The large decorative motif betrays the Moorish heritage in this Muslim part of West Central Africa. The influence of Arab traders, and the ornamental detail on the leather and carved goods with which they bartered, can be seen in many parts of the continent, particularly the east coast.

INDIA

It was in the Indian sub-continent that colour came of age. Confident and unfettered colour use seems the birthright of the Indian people. The brashest of hues look bright and gay under the blazing sun. Indian arts and crafts, both traditional and modern, decorative and practical, natural or stylized, have a common theme of vivid, even gaudy, coloration.

Colour is an integral part of Hindu worship. Vermilion and ochre represent blood in sacrificial rites; brides are sprinkled with turmeric; yellow clothes are worn and yellow food eaten at the spring festivals, to symbolize the ripening of the crops. Outside many temples, merchants preside over stalls ranged with bowls containing heaps of bright pigments. Worshippers buy them to paint their faces before taking part in religious ceremonies. At the festival of Holi, which celebrates the visit to earth of the great Krishna, god of all aspects of love, people gaily throw coloured powder and water over one another.

This innocent joy in colour is appropriate in a culture where its brilliance has become the property of the people. Wherever there are mass gatherings, at ceremonial occasions or merely in the market, there is a riot of colour, a festive chaos that acclaims individuality and defies any question of vulgarity. The brilliance of saturated hues, shot with gold and silver thread or decoration, shimmers in the intensity of the sunlight. It has been said that in dress 'shocking pink is the navy blue of India' but, although apposite, this denies the rich diversity of Indian colour – betraying a sensibility of enormous sophistication and a facility of self-expression through colour that defies convention.

There is evidence that the interiors of the houses of the sub-continent have been painted in such bright colours since the seventh century BC; that tradition lingers on, seemingly undiminished, to the present day.

Gold, silver and electric blue sweet wrappings have been cut and pasted on a length of pink muslin fabric, to produce an inexpensively elegant decorative wall hanging. Such unabashed mimicry of the elaborate trappings of an aristocratic interior are common in all regions and amongst all classes.

Traditional Indian dyes and dyeing techniques vary so much from region to region that the colours of a woman's sari tell the expert eye from which part of the sub-continent she comes. Traditional dyeing methods extract from native plants and insects colours as bright as those produced by modern synthetic dyes, so the peacock blues and shocking pinks of these saris are as distinctly Indian as the rich earth reds and saffron yellows.

A detail from an eighteenth-century painting from Udaipur vividly illustrates the richness and range of colours and the bold deployment of pattern with pattern that is characteristic of all levels of culture on the sub-continent. The piercing hues of the sky and the myriad colours of the landscape, flora and fauna are mirrored everywhere in Indian daily life.

The nobleman in the painting wears white, ritually associated with the Brahmin, or highest caste, while his sword-carrier is garbed in the red that is symbolic of the warrior classes.

THE AMERICAN INDIAN

The 'West' was only 'Wild' to European newcomers. What they saw as wilderness, wild animals and savages appeared to the Indians as a bountiful land wherein they dwelt in perfect harmony with Nature. Indian crafts quickly developed a highly stylized use of pattern and colour to symbolize the elements of their surroundings; the earth's reds and browns, the blues and black of the sky; the white of water, and the green of foliage.

In this blissful state, the Indians possessed only a rudimentary sense of time: the cycle of day and night. They had no words for times of the day or the days themselves. Colour became a means of expressing time. The varying light of the sun at different times of the day or the changing hues of trees with the seasons were depicted as a record of a particular moment.

Essentially nomadic tribes, the Indians of North America concentrated their considerable decorative skills on their body-painting, clothing and artefacts: elaborate beadwork and quill-stitching on animal skins; the refined geometry of woven blankets and rugs and finely constructed and embellished basketwork.

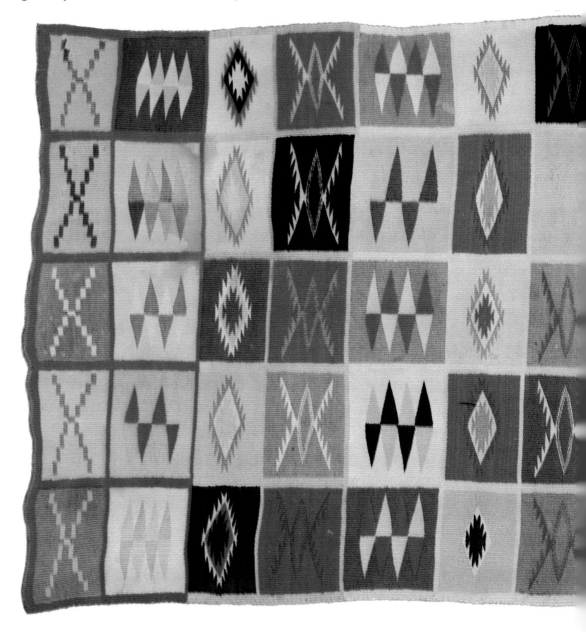

Warpaint and Redskins go together in most minds, fed on the myths of 'westerns'. Young warriors also wore elaborate beadwork endowed with great ritual symbolism. Early tubular beads, or *wampum*, were made from clam shells and dyed in a restrained range of colours: white and azure predominating. Such sobriety was held to be an outward sign of the composure and serenity that the tribes encouraged.

The Navaho rug originally used only plain stripes of indigo against undyed wool, copying the designs of the Hopi and Zuni tribes, from whom they had learned the techniques of weaving. When commercially spun wool, called 'Germantown' in America, and brightly coloured modern aniline dyes reached them via the trading posts, in the late nineteenth century, more vigorous designs and bolder colours were employed. The diamond and triangle motifs are poetic stylizations of the canyons and plateaux of their surroundings. The use of black and red in such a grid symbolizes earth.

However, they did also paint both the inside and outside of their *tipis* (usually made of animal hides) with pictographic representations of battles or buffalo hunts. It was also common to depict memorable dreams in this way for it was thought to bring great fortune to the *tipi* inhabitants. Indians changed homes frequently, and such tents developed a high resale value, since this magic was held to be transferable.

The mystical presence of Nature in Indian decoration gives it a forceful and stimulating directness.

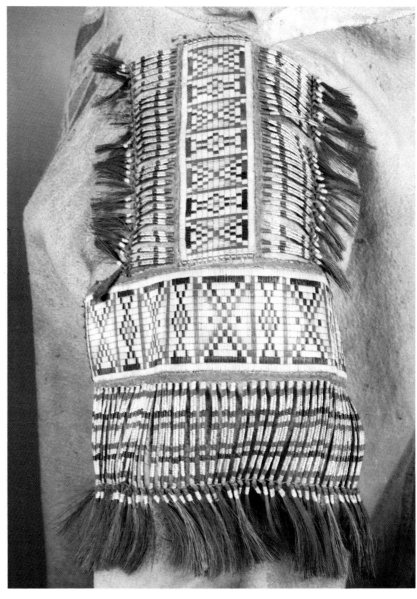

The quillwork of the plains Indians is an ancient sewing technique, dating back as far as the fourteenth century. Porcupine quills, strands of moosehair, or even quills from birds, were dyed and then softened by being worked in the mouth. This Cree shirt uses beads and quills on the fringing. Initially quills were coloured only cream, orange, brown or black, using natural dyes. As trade with the white man grew, red, green and blue began to appear and, eventually, for export and tourist trade, they took to using vivid and gaudy shades in vibrant patterns. The fine translucent sheen of the naturally dyed quills is, however, the perfect foil for the fine-grained texture of the buckskin of the shirt. The use of abstract triangle and box shapes and stepped lines, on either a white or blue ground, came to the Cree from the neighbouring Western Sioux.

LATIN AMERICA

South of the border, things heat up – insistent sun, spicy food, volatile passions and everything ablaze with totally uninhibited colour. The colour heritage of Latin America is ancient, rich and riotous. Surviving artefacts of the great early civilizations reveal a delight in the most spectacular chromatic intensity that combined art and Nature could afford. The Incas and Aztecs created fabulous head-dresses, capes and other adornments of featherwork and mosaic. The shimmering plumage of exotic birds from the tropical rain forest arrayed the nobility, while masks, exquisitely encrusted with turquoise, serpentine, malachite and shell, served

ceremonial purposes. The impact of the conquering Spaniards, however devastating in other ways, did not diminish the New World's appetite for brilliance for Spain's own colour tradition was formidable. The *conquistadores* were amazed by the native's fabric techniques – brocade, embroidery, tapestry-work – many of which proved more skilled than in Europe. The intricate designs in cotton and wool, dyed vibrant colours, often had cult significance.

Today's more peaceful visitors to Latin America are still impressed with the weaving, beading and embroidery displayed to attract the tourist. Primitive motifs, evocative of children's drawings, look best in the bold tones that the young prefer. Traditional costume is still much in evidence, not merely to divert visitors, but to express the people's abiding love for colours as luminous as ethnic neon. The exaggerated brightness and breath-taking tonal gradations of such wares as rugs, mats, blankets or enormous paper flowers give zest to an existence that can, in other respects, be sleepy, tedious or just plain poor.

Anywhere the sun shines relentlessly, only the strongest colours can hold their own. They are spontaneously imitative of abundant flowers, and flattering to the dark complexions associated with such climes.

As an influence on modern decorating, they have a special place. The costumes, textiles and artefacts, which look appropriate *in situ*, pounce visually from import shops in chilly climes. They are overwhelming when massed, but can make dramatic focal points in either a largely monochromatic or compatibly contrasting scheme. As a bedside rug, wall hanging, part of a collage, trimmings for special occasions – whether used temporarily or permanently – these chromatic fireworks can spark a *fiesta* atmosphere.

A young Peruvian woman, resplendent in the national costume still worn for high-days, holidays and carnivals, displays colours that are a celebration in themselves. There is a jubilant, heaped-up effect from the sheer multiplicity of clothing items and patterns – rick-rack and ribbon-trimmed hat; stripey shawl; embroidered cloak, blouse and skirt.

Tufts of wool, brilliantly dyed in fuschia, purple, chrome yellow, crimson and bright green, make a festive boa in tones matched by the woven shawl's clear stripes.

Exuberant, highly saturated colour on this Mexican souvenir stall dazzles the eye. The staggering effect is heightened by the contrast of strong sunlight and deep shadow. The appeal of these handwoven rugs and mats is in the suitability of the naïve images – sun, flowers, birds, wheels – to the wild vitality of the pulsating primaries.

JAPAN

The gentle genius of Japanese design lies in a formality utterly free of pretension. Ritual once pervaded every aspect of life, defining the style we have come to recognize as classically Japanese – rectangular lines; natural tones and textures; and large areas of varied neutrals, galvanized by precisely placed focal points of vivid colour. Tranquillity – the antithesis of artifice – was the goal of these free-floating interiors.

The traditional *sukiya* style evolved in the fourteenth century, when the ruling classes chose to temper palatial excess with rustic austerity. The venerable qualities of *sabi* (evidence of antiquity) and *wabi* (the subdued note of solitude), which characterized the tea ceremony, were assimilated into domestic architecture. The dwellings of rich and poor had a surprising amount in common: an intimacy with Nature permitted by movable walls; the shrine-like *tokonoma* recess with its varying display of scrolls, flowering branches or sublime ceramics; and the woven *tatami* mats used for sitting and lying, which became the standard unit of measure for houses. Rectangles dominated everything, from the floor plan to the carefully proportioned subdivisions of wall space, to garments made of flat, angular panels.

Respect for natural materials made neutrals the rule for interiors; access to quantities of handsome timber – firs, cedars, pines, cypresses – gave prominence to wood tones and textures, However, the chief ornament of the indoors remained the outdoors. Sliding walls made garden vistas integral parts of interiors otherwise monolithically plain, apart from the *tokonoma*.

Elements of Japanese style were embraced by the West from the mid-nineteenth century onwards, as a result of exposure through trade and international exhibitions. *Japonisme*, the cultural rage of Paris in the late 1800s, was inspired by glorious examples of their decorative and fine arts, whereas later Bauhaus design can be linked with the minimalist, form-follows-function aspect of Japanese architecture.

The West adapted Japan's economical use of space, conservative coloration and harmony with Nature; sliding glass doors and panoramic picture windows recall movable paper walls. The principles of line, light and texture, prized for centuries in Japan, are now a source of peace and beauty to all the modern world.

Slender branches of flowering cherry beautify a quiet corner. The delicate shapes and tender shades of pink are an exquisite foil for the heavy-textured ceramics and greeny-beige surroundings. In this simple context, even the scattering of petals looks purposeful and poetic, rather than disorderly. The profound impact of so little bright colour bears out the 'less is more' doctrine; the same arrangement would almost certainly be swamped in a Western scheme of traditional chintzes and billowing bouquets.

Although restraint and humility are keynotes of the highly ritualized Japanese tea ceremony, colour is permitted in dress. In the classic Edo period, dyeing took precedence over weaving, with emphasis on strong, clear colours. Here a rich crimson kimono imparts majesty and joy to the occasion of which it is a focal point. Again, the austerity of the setting makes an even greater feature of this bold chromatic stroke. Contrast in texture, as much as tone, is another staple of Japanese decoration: the coarse weave of the golden *tatami* mats against a glossy black lacquer; gleaming glaze teamed with the flat translucence of the paper screen.

This farmhouse embodies the natural grace and integrity that so attracted Japan's ruling classes from the fourteenth century onward. In rejecting the Chinese style they regarded as grandiose, they embraced rural simplicity, redefining town houses – and even palaces – with prominence given to the country qualities of light and pure texture. Here tranquillity abounds, generated by the unadorned elements – wood, stone, fire, paper, rush mats. The prevailing coloration is subdued and neutral. Even the banners hung over the front door are in sober tones, suitable to their strong, interlocking motif of protective significance. The aggregate effect of all the neutral surfaces – lightest at floor level and darker toward the ceiling – is to create an interior of spontaneous, unforced unity, and spiritual peace.

How colour works

We usually consider colour in terms of things – a spectacular sunset, a Monet masterpiece, even blue suede shoes; and we name or describe colours according to evocative associations – burgundy red, canary yellow, jade green. But the truth about colour is that it has no physical substance, not even in dyes and pigments. It is simply and entirely waves of light.

Colour theory considers the spectral hues and their influence on one another, as well as their effect upon us. Instead of using picturesque names, it defines colours scientifically according to hue (position in the spectrum), value (the white or black content, determining lightness or darkness) and chroma, or saturation (relative purity or greyness). The colour wheel is a graphic reference to related and contrasting hues, warm and cool combinations, and the relationship of the primary colours to secondaries, tertiaries and their complementaries. A grasp of these is a great aid in planning the scheme you want – stimulating or serene, cosy or chic.

Gain valuable insight into the dynamic range of the main colour groups by making your own collections. Professional colour consultants use anything from pinboards to old shoe boxes to build up a colour story from scraps of fabric, carpet, wallpaper, paint swatches, magazine tearsheets, commercial packaging – 'colorabilia' from buttons to bottle-caps. This easy, gradual and fun exercise will raise your colour consciousness, improving your appreciation of what remarkably different personalities colours possess. See how to make a mixture of patterns compatible; how to alter the appearance of a room's size and shape. Once you learn how colour works, you will enjoy meeting new challenges.

The industrious primary colours share the honours in a London architect's award-winning celebration of the work ethic: an early showpiece of high-tech.

THE COLOUR WHEEL

Colour is no less magical for being properly understood. If you already enjoy an instinctive approach to decorating, the colour wheel may appear academic or superfluous. But if you rely exclusively on a romantic notion of colour, you risk getting hit or miss results with your schemes. Just as a person who sings harmony by ear can still benefit by learning to read music, so the intuitive home decorator gains by absorbing at least the rudiments of colour theory.

The mere dozen hues on the colour wheels below are not intended as candidates for your next interior. After all, the human eye can distinguish some 10 million variations of colour. What makes the wheel an invaluable tool is the graphic reference it provides as to which *families* of colours harmonize and which contrast, which are warm and which are cool.

The wheel is a circular arrangement of colours following the same order as the spectrum, but joining the violet at the far end back to the red at the front end. The brainchild of seventeenth-century physicist, Sir Isaac Newton, it places all related colours near to one another with exactly contrasting, or, 'complementary', colours directly opposite them. Complementary pairs are those which, when mixed together in the same proportion, produce grey (except in the case of coloured light, where such a mixture produces white). When you place complementary colours, such as red and green, side by side, they appear to the eye virtually to vibrate. Stare fixedly at any colour for a minute; when you look away or blink, its complement appears as an after-image. The wheel groups the warm, colours – reds, oranges and yellows – opposite the cool blues, greens and violets.

Colour has no tangible existence: it is how we perceive various waves of light. What we think of as plain, white light – ordinary daylight – is composed of every colour in the spectrum. You can see white light broken into its spectral constituent bands of red, orange, yellow, green, blue and violet with the aid of a prism or, naturally, in a rainbow, when the droplets of moisture in the air act like a prism. The colour of almost everything is determined by the wavelengths of light it absorbs. However, we never see what is absorbed; we see only what is reflected. For example, a London bus absorbs all but the red wavelengths. Because of their varying wavelengths, colours are focused in different ways by the lens of the eye. This partly explains why hues from the long-wavelength, red end of the spectrum are described as 'advancing', and those from the short-wavelength, violet end as 'receding'.

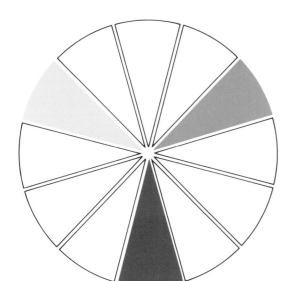

Red, yellow and blue are the primary colours. They cannot be created by mixing other colours; they are entirely pure. It is by mixing them that all other colours are produced. If you mix all three equally, you get grey. The primaries are naturally equidistant on the colour wheel, dividing it into thirds. Their attention-getting showiness appeals to the young in particular, and to the bold-spirited.

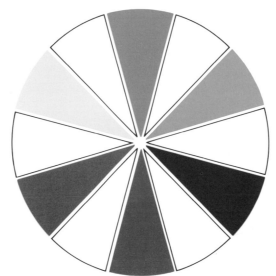

Orange, green and violet are the secondary colours, each produced by an equal mixture of two of the primaries either side of them on the colour wheel – red and yellow for orange, blue and yellow for green, blue and red for violet. Each is the complementary colour of the one primary not used in its make-up, and sits opposite it. With the primaries, they compose the basic spectrum.

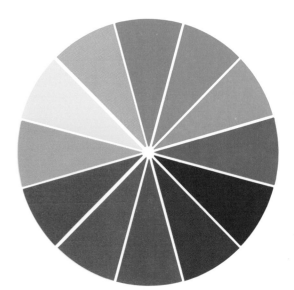

A tertiary is a colour mixture containing equal parts of a primary and its flanking secondary, so that you get orange-red, blue-green and so on. The primaries, secondaries and tertiaries make up the standard colour wheel. They give just a suggestion of the infinite number of gradations achieved by mixing varying amounts of either neighbouring colours or any two of the primaries.

Each segment of the colour wheel represents a vast family of tints and shades, with relatives ranging – in the case of red alone – from a barely perceptible pink to an almost black maroon, and everything from flaming scarlets to dusky, faded roses in between. Colours are assessed according to three characteristics: hue, which indicates a colour's position on the wheel and gives it its name; value or lightness, which tells how much white or black it contains, and chroma, or saturation, which is a measure of purity or intensity. Thus a pinky, dove-grey is low in chroma and high in value; crimson is highly saturated, medium in value.

The colour wheel shows only hue. To include lightness and saturation, and to understand the relationship of all three attributes, it helps to imagine what is called a colour solid. Its vertical axis, showing lightness, is white at the 'north pole' darkening through a series of greys to black at the 'south pole'; the 'equator' consists of the pure hues in their spectral order – just like the colour wheel. Saturation is the horizontal axis, like a spoke coming from the neutral, grey centre, getting ever brighter as it nears its purest level at the rim. Using just these three co-ordinates, any colour can be precisely defined.

When planning a colour scheme, take notice of the lightness and saturation of the colours you choose; they are as important as hue for getting the compatibility – or calculated contrast – you want. They can also be the reason why certain combinations are unflattering. If one colour is subtly greyed (designers sometimes say 'dirty'), it may look discredited next to a singingly clear tone. The same colour, seen with companions of similar value – say misty taupes, cloudy violets – can be heavenly. Textures, finishes and lighting affect colour, so always ensure that you check paint, paper and fibres *in situ*.

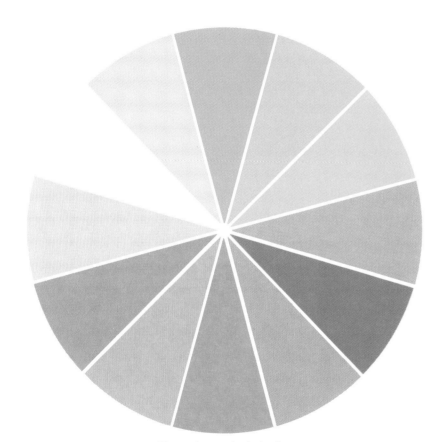

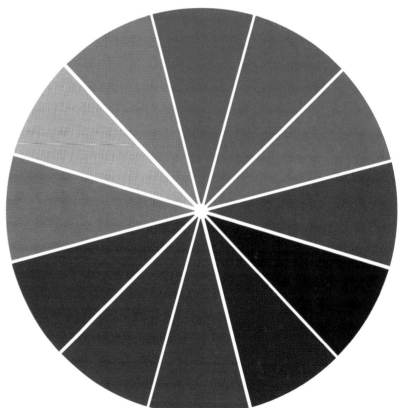

This is the standard wheel with 50% white added so as to lighten the colours in the direction of pastels. Colours with white added are designated 'tints'. The palest pastels all blend harmoniously – even opposites on the wheel.

In this wheel, 50% black has been added to produce a darkened range of colours known as 'shades', the term for any colour to which black is added. Oddly, dark shades have no common name analogous to pastels, describing lighter tints.

HARMONY AND CONTRAST

There are two basic categories of interior colour schemes – related and contrasting. Related schemes may be either 'monochromatic' (various shades of the same colour – powder- to cornflower- to navy-blue, for instance) or 'analogous' (harmonizing colours from adjacent sections of the wheel, such as a lime yellow-green, a dark holly-green and a turquoise blue-green). Because monochromatic and analogous schemes are based on close colour families, they tend to be distinctly either warm or cool, unless they emphasize yellow-greens or red-violets, which are of an intermediate psychological 'temperature'.

Contrasting schemes employ the dynamic complementaries. It may be a simple pair – yellow and violet, expressed as pale primrose and rich iris purple, with intermediate golds or lilacs added for depth; or a 'double complementary' pair, twinning the yellow with yellow-orange and the violet with blue-violet.

A 'split complementary' mates a hue with the two hues flanking its complement – say a blue with a red-orange and a yellow-orange. 'Triad' schemes use three colours equidistant on the wheel – the primaries or secondaries, for instance. 'Tetrads', which take four colours equidistant on the wheel (hence two diverse complementary pairs) – say orange and blue, yellow-green and red-violet – produce ambitious, complex schemes.

Differences in the value and saturation of selected colours, and in the proportions in which they are used, make possible unlimited versions of any basic decorating scheme.

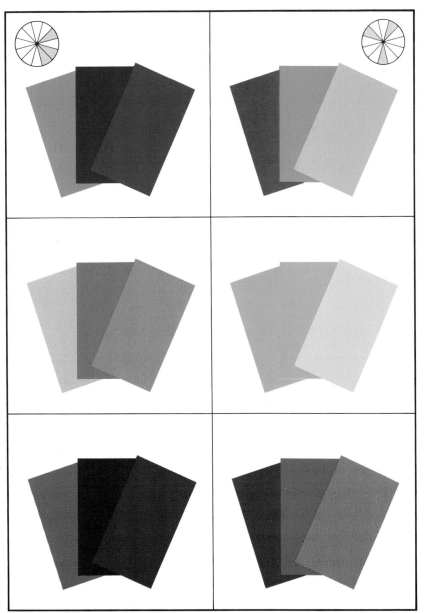

Study these examples of harmony and contrast. Few are strictly precise triads, split complementaries and so on; rather, they illustrate how such themes may be subtly interpreted and still retain the desired characteristics of their general category.

The small pie-charts show the sections on the colour wheels, on the previous pages, to which these samples correspond. Where the shaded areas are closely grouped, the trios are harmoniously related; where they are wide apart, the colours are contrasting.

The blue, violet and red-violet trio skips the space that would have made it perfectly analogous, but it is still obviously related – an adventurous harmony.

The red, blue-green and yellow is almost a primary triad, but it is given a lively twist by substituting blue-green for blue. The clear contrast is biased in favour of the two warm shades, but in practice the balance could be reversed by using these as small accents in a largely blue-green room.

The red, red-orange and orange hot-spot is a classic analogous set – one primary, one tertiary, one secondary – for a flowing, uninterrupted harmony. No matter what order they appear in when used together, the combined effect will be of a sweet, strong colour chord.

In every example, if you 'read' each colour vertically through the lightened and darkened sets, you see sample monochrome trios.

Blue and yellow seen side by side are a bright contrast, but when separated by silvery grey they begin to harmonize. This is the peace-making, catalytic function of an achromatic neutral. Because grey is in effect a 'colourless colour', it relates equally to both of these strong primaries and eases the visual transition between them.

Blue, red and blue-green – a sparkling combination, fit for Chinese silks – make a dynamically contrasting trio. Although there are no exact, complementary pairings, as either a more orangey red or a true green would have provided, there is still a singing contrast, with the warm red easily holding its own, although flanked by the two cooler shades.

Yellow, yellow-green and green are a brilliant analogous series of sharp, citrus shades. They show that a harmonious scheme is not automatically passive, as compared to active complementaries. This trio has plenty of bite. The combination is from the intermediate temperature range, bridging warm and cool.

Yellow, blue-violet and yellow-green have the fresh, clear contrast of spring flowers and foliage. The yellow and blue-violet are practically complementary, giving the trio its verve. Hue is not the only contrast; there is a strong element of light and dark. With one warm, one cool and one intermediate shade, the temperature averages out.

In all the combinations shown, it will be noted that the addition of either black or white to the original colours makes both the related and the contrasting series more harmonious. That is because the colours now have their matching content of light or dark in common. It is a reliable means of ensuring compatibility.

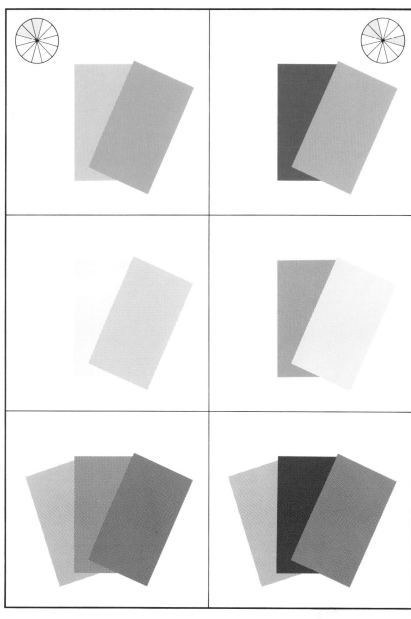

GETTING THE BLUES

As faint as a puff of smoke, or as deep as the night sky – blue has an incredible range, and is so perennially popular we seem never to have a surfeit of it. Vast expanses of sea and sky accommodate the spirit craving release through a sense of infinity; their depth and loftiness have endowed their colour with a noble character. Blue makes a room cool and peaceable. It agrees so well with other colours that it functions as the most nearly neutral of the primaries, yet it retains its' own identity with ease.

The irresistible magic of blue radiates from many a pair of eyes, a peacock's neck, a royal sapphire, a priceless ancient painting of the Madonna's mantle – its pigment processed from treasured lapis lazuli. Art and Nature abound with inspirations for the colours you can collect yourself – in fabric and carpet swatches, plastics, china, paper and paint chips.

Blues can stray toward either of their neighbours in the spectrum – namely greens and violets – according to the amount of yellow or red they contain. They vary, too, in clarity, depending on how much black, white or grey is in them. In decorating, the chalkier, diffuse blues lend themselves to large surfaces; while the intense blues work well as accents or in specific dramatic effects.

Which room should be blue? The 'Blue Room' in the song by Rodgers and Hart was a honeymooners' bower. In addition to its romantic connotation, a blue bedroom (especially darker blue) is reputed to enhance one's ability to remember dreams. Blue can make the living-room airy, spacious and calm. In the bathroom, blue is both cleanly and evocative of water. It is traditional in kitchens, both in tiles and on china. It can also present an ultra-modern, high-tech appearance. Remember when using blue that it can be chilly, especially in a room facing away from the sun. Conversely, it is just the colour to make a hot spot seem temperate.

Blue is universally beloved because it flatters nearly everyone, but take care not to pigeon-hole it in your mind on the basis of a favourite garment. Your collection can span the wide range from the powder-soft to the electric. Study the hues carefully. Somewhere in there is the precise colour of heaven.

GOING FOR GREENS

Greens are a matter of life and death – from the vital gleam of lush foliage to the murk of mould and decay. Green is Nature's number one colour, and in decorating terms it provides the means of bringing the outdoors in.

Growing greenery runs the gamut from pale, misty lichen to the inky gloss of holly and ivy. In between are numberless permutations of the colour occurring in grasses, stems and leaves. Because we are conditioned to seeing a multitude of greens coexisting in harmony, green is an ideal choice for a room scheme built around variations of one basic colour, with no need for strict matching. Green patterns are always pleasant underfoot.

Pliny's ancient observation that 'Emerald delights the eye without fatiguing it,' has been vindicated by the later discovery that green light focuses almost exactly on the retina. This soothing quality is why, for more than three hundred years, theatres have offered the backstage sanctuary, known as the Green Room to actors awaiting call or entertaining friends.

Decorating provides a creative way to indulge our instinctive visual appetite for green, making up for the fact that it can be a tricky colour to wear. In collecting green you will encounter certain of the most subtle shades in the history of the decorative arts: the elusive, hypnotic grey-green-blue known as celadon, introduced to the West by Sung dynasty porcelain; and its descendant, the delicate neo-classic Adam green, whose popularity led, alas, to the debased version we nowadays unofficially recognize (and shun) as 'institutional green'.

For inspiration, look to Cézanne's outdoor paintings, or the rich, brooding jungle greens of Henri Rousseau. Consider the mood of the room you want to decorate; the light or sharp greens are intrinsically youthful; the moss, avocado and olive tones are more mature and satisfying.

Because green forms the backcloth to all things floral, it contrasts well with pinks and reds. It complements its cool partner blue, and harmonizes with pastels and turquoise. Green, whether tart, minty or darkly crisp, is prized for sheer freshness. No wonder city dwellers devise oases in the concrete desert by the skilful application of a decorative green thumb.

SAY YES TO YELLOWS

Yellow has been trapped in the kitchen nearly as long as women have but, in the same way, can also work wonders out of it, given the chance. The master colourist Monet positively filled his dining-room with yellow's beaming charm; a yellow bed-room could even make getting up a matter of optimism.

An intangible yellow is, quite literally, what lights up our lives, as both the rays of morning or evening sun and the most common form of artificial light, from incandescent bulbs, brim with yellow wave-lengths. Our association of yellow with sun is so strong we inevitably think of it as a morning-time-of-day, summer-time-of-year colour. This instinctive bias has made the fashion for yellow markedly greater in and around the tropics than in cool, cloudy climates.

True yellow is psychologically the happiest colour in the spectrum, but people often shy away from it because it can be hard to handle. Both yellow and orange are rapidly perceived, which explains their prevalence in commercial packaging, and applications relating to emergencies and safety. This showiness may persuade people that this is not a fit colour to live with or that, as verified physiologi-cally, a little of it goes a long way; however, there remain legions of amenable yellows which possess a cheerful disposition without being overpowering. A dash of yellow in a pot of white paint takes the chill off, giving a warm, creamy shade suitable for any room in the house.

There are three broad categories of yellow commonly used by decorators: the clear, bold citrus and spring-flower tones, with their astringent, en-ergizing effect for a sunny, youthful look; the copper, brass and gilt metallics for an opulent, formal appearance; and the earthy ochres used in conjunction with other neutrals for a simple, but warm, architectural treatment.

The colours which emerge as yellow advances along the spectrum to bright orange are difficult to use in large solid quantities, but have just the right impact when used as accents or as ingredients in prints and patterns. Orange has tropical, exotic qualities, but also lends itself well to the most utilitarian, plastic kitchen and housekeeping items.

As you collect these uplifting shades, look around your house to see which room is most in need of a smile.

ROLL OUT THE REDS

Red says 'Look at me!' louder than words. It is the supercolour of the spectrum – bold, imperative, provocative. If you love it, and want to use a lot of it, think in terms of action – of entertaining or dining-rooms. Restaurants often have red décor because it stimulates both the appetite and the conversation. Red's physical effect is such that exposure to quantities of it prompts the release of adrenalin into the bloodstream, quickens the heart rate and engenders a sense of warmth. Its unmatched impact has recommended its signal use to fields as diverse as heraldry and harlotry: roll out the red carpet; turn on the red light.

To all ages and cultures, red's primary association is with blood. Rage, passion or courage – all's red in love and war. In nature, however, we rarely see broad canvasses of red: even tropical sunsets are multi-hued and tend towards red's offspring, purple and orange. Red occurs, rather, as an accent – a cluster of ripe fruit, scattered roadside poppies, a cardinal bird in winter woods.

The use of red in interiors is more appropriate to sophisticated city settings than to country cottages, but a traditional touch like the classic red-and-white-checked table-cloth is synonymous with cheerful, informal eating.

As with the other primaries, the high-tech movement has made use of red's vivid connotations to colour code and transform the most functional objects – hot water pipes, cable wire – into focal points. For related reasons, red has appealed to modern painters like Calder, Mondrian, and Lichtenstein. A few lipstick-red features give the kiss of life to a comatose scheme.

Red creates excitement. Red *dares*. Its use suggests confidence and has historically coincided with flourishing cultures – Pompeian walls, Regency stripes. Be sure your collection includes such rich variations as russets and burgundies.

We talk about – and can visualize – light green and light blue, say; but pink is so utterly different in its attributes from red that it requires a name of its own. For decorators, pink can be extremely pleasure-giving – blissful, gentle, luxurious. Too strong a pink may be sickly when used in bulk, but a well-chosen pastel can ameliorate a dimly- or coldly-aspected room. Try it, and you won't need rose-tinted glasses.

KNOW YOUR NEUTRALS

Never dismiss neutrals as dull but necessary; they are the decorator's work-horse. You will almost certainly be using them again and again; so learn to differentiate their individual characteristics. Although any neutral should, by definition, coexist happily with more dominant shades, there are specific neutrals which show various spectral hues to maximum advantage.

Strictly speaking, neutrals are achromatic, but in practice the term embraces the families of browns and beiges, of off-whites such as bone or ivory, and of tinted greys, as well as the standard white to grey to black.

Neutrals have both an international and an eternal quality which makes them at once the most primitive and the most futuristic of tones – mud huts and space shuttles. Neutrals are also the epitome of both town and country looks – from wicker, matting and pine to smoked mirrors, black leather and chrome.

Neutrals are to a large extent naturals – earth, stone, wood, straw, ice, sand, pebbles, hides, shells; but they also represent the man-made world of metal, glass and concrete. They celebrate function in both domestic and business contexts. In the last two or three decades the 'executive office' look has successfully infiltrated the home, but it cries out for the personal touch by way of imaginative accents.

Neutrals are perennially popular for certain obvious reasons. They are supremely practical in that they age with grace. A bit of venerable dirt or fading will not spoil their looks and can even enhance them. They are peaceful to live with and offend no one. For such reasons, timid or deliberately conservative decorators seek safety in umbers. A more positive virtue of neutrals is the way in which they set off a prize painting, rug or flower arrangement – they also serve who only stand and make something else look good.

Neutrals, too, supply a treasure trove of textures, as anyone who has painstakingly stripped a fine old door or floor will attest.

The achromatic neutrals have a ritual significance for us; white and/or black see us through christenings, weddings, funerals and random formal occasions in between. Always classic, dramatic, correct, they carry these qualities into schemes where they are emphasized.

Once you have control of neutrals, you can put any scheme into top gear.

PATTERNS AND PLAINS

Basing a colour scheme on a prominently used pattern, such as a carpet or upholstery print, may sound unoriginal, but you can play it in any way you like – for harmony or contrast, serenity or drama, intimacy or spaciousness. Sofas are obvious starting points; they are big investments, and usually the most prominent use of pattern in the room.

Repeating the pattern with matching wallpaper or curtains will tie a large room together, or keep a small room snug. Conversely, using paler solid tones from the print on the walls will enhance the sense of space.

For a traditional, balanced look, match the colours in the print and use them in the same proportion. Manufacturers often supply the full range – coordinating wallpaper and fabric, or paints and solid-colour fabrics keyed to the print.

You can also start from scratch with a swatch of your upholstery fabric. If one is not available, cut a small piece from the underside of the sofa, or resort to a commercial colour reference such as the 'Pantone' books of colour chips.

To test colours properly, you must see them *in situ*. Using the small tester pots, paint a generous patch either directly on the wall (behind the sofa, if the sofa is against a wall) or on a large sheet of paper you can fix to the wall. This way you can try several colours at the same time and even move them around to see how they look in different parts of the room. Carpets can be evaluated only on the floor; try a sample piece under the front leg of the sofa. Live with the test colours for a good forty-eight hours in both natural and artificial light, so that you can check for 'metamerism' – the effect whereby, paint and fabric colours which look identical in daylight, do not match under electric light. Remember, too, that a paper sample is an inadequate reference for materials whose textures are subject to light and shadow.

If you prefer dark walls for a dramatic effect, try a gloss finish. Its sheen will reflect the light that matt surfaces simply devour. If you choose white for walls, soften it with a drop of the print ground-colour, as fabric white is invariably 'off' compared to dead-white paint.

Here six sofas are matched with swatches that could be used interchangeably for carpet, curtains, walls, additional upholstery and accessories. Even these permutations are just a beginning: stimulating suggestions to whet your imagination.

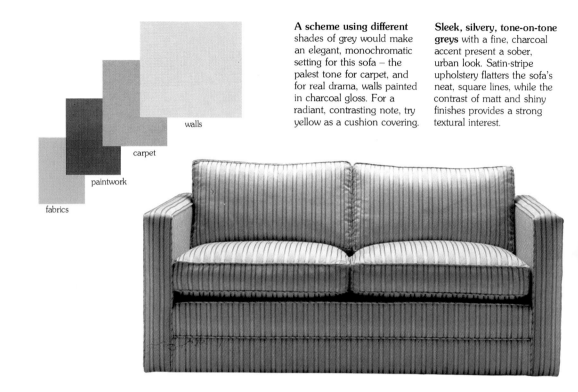

walls

carpet

paintwork

fabrics

A scheme using different shades of grey would make an elegant, monochromatic setting for this sofa – the palest tone for carpet, and for real drama, walls painted in charcoal gloss. For a radiant, contrasting note, try yellow as a cushion covering.

Sleek, silvery, tone-on-tone greys with a fine, charcoal accent present a sober, urban look. Satin-stripe upholstery flatters the sofa's neat, square lines, while the contrast of matt and shiny finishes provides a strong textural interest.

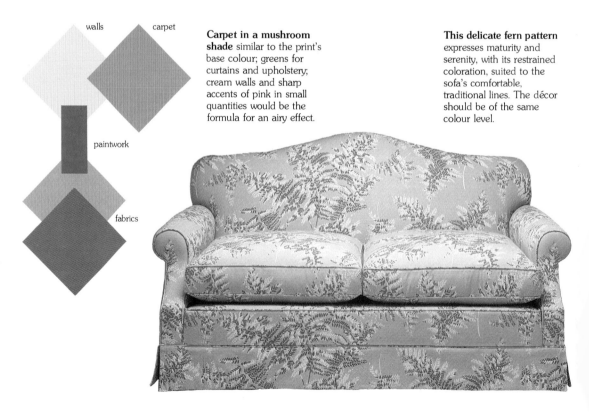

walls

carpet

paintwork

fabrics

Carpet in a mushroom shade similar to the print's base colour; greens for curtains and upholstery; cream walls and sharp accents of pink in small quantities would be the formula for an airy effect.

This delicate fern pattern expresses maturity and serenity, with its restrained coloration, suited to the sofa's comfortable, traditional lines. The décor should be of the same colour level.

A sheaf of summery blues, normally associated with sea, sky and boats, here lends its cooling touch to a tropical foliage motif. The luxury of a white carpet could be justified in a refreshing blue and white scheme, with luscious accents of soft red.

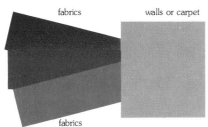

fabrics

walls or carpet

fabrics

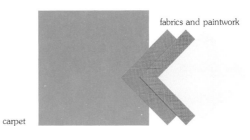

fabrics and paintwork

carpet

The joys of spring abound in this print where greens and yellows predominate, and where all the colours are given breathing space on the generous white ground. It would suit a morning room with green carpet, warmed-white walls and accents of the other print colours.

The gentle, greyed pastels of this bargello print have an accessible elegance – the soft, multicoloured look is both pretty and chic. The flexibility of pastels is such that nearly any colour of the same value could be part of the scheme – peach walls, grey carpet, green or blue drapes.

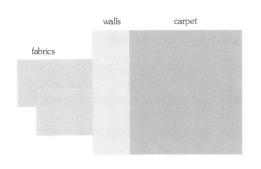

fabrics

walls

carpet

paintwork

carpet

walls

fabrics

This earthy-rich tapestry floral gives off a golden glow. It is strong enough to balance a dramatic scheme: perhaps walls painted one of the deeper print colours with a gloss finish, and carpet in pale blue – taking the heat off the ensemble while bringing out one of the sofa's subtler colours.

53

PATTERN IN THE ABSTRACT

Mixing patterns, using assorted geometrics and stripes in conjunction, might sound controversial – the jarring vision of a room clownishly attired in graphic clashes. However, as in any case where unwritten laws of style are broken, colour can bend the rules with superb results.

The trick is to select patterns which relate to one another, using the same tones in approximately the same proportions, or in permutations chosen for a deliberate contrast. The mixture then becomes organic, rather than frenetic, producing a scheme of exceptional resonance and depth.

Finding patterns within the same colour family is not difficult. When looking through any fabric- or wallpaper-company's swatches for the season, you will see a series of designs, each offered in a choice of colour-ways, so that the background shade of one is the accent shade of another. From pattern to pattern, it is likely the same company is using the same dyes, so the French blue in their geometric print, for instance, will be the same as the French blue in their stripes – and might well be available as a plain solid.

Using your chosen basic colours as the link, you can easily round up a harmonious batch of furnishing fabrics, wall and floor coverings and accessories. Remember that fashion colours are usually co-ordinated industry-wide, from season to season, so at any time you can expect to collect all the ingredients necessary to round off your interior schemes.

Consider the dynamic aspect of patterns in terms of colour and line. A large-scale, pastel print will feel calm; a small-scale, bright print will look busy. In mixing patterns, what is called 'scale value' can be an interesting link – using the same design in varying sizes.

Plain solids, as well as random or all-over designs, make good bridges between geometrics and stripes. So long as the colours relate, all manner of patterns can work happily together.

Half a dozen different patterns, united by their common use of blues and off-white, have a breath-taking aggregate impact, giving the room a fantasy, stage-set air.

The crisply picked-out mouldings and cornices share a geometric style with the carpet, in contrast to the moiré striped pattern of the fabric in the alcove, the random design of the marble-effect baseboards, the 'op-art' table-cloth and traditional blue-and-white china.

Two shades of blue have been used to accentuate the classical detail of the door-frames and moulding, in a way that relates directly to the painted navy-blue highlights of the cream-coloured chairs.

Drapes of the earthy-brown linen, finely striped in brick-red and teal-blue, would contrast well with cream-ground walls.

An American-Indian inspired, geometric wallpaper design of a lightened turquoise and terracotta motif on cream is the basis for a scheme, which is accented with richer versions of its constituent colours, expressed in both stripes and solids.

Complementary patterns – one a semi-abstract floral stripe wallpaper, the other a classic, large-scale floral upholstery fabric – could be teamed effectively, due to their joint use of rust, beige and French blue on a dark ground.

Nubbly, multicoloured tweed upholstery is an excellent textural foil, complemented by the rich burgundy carpet, which, alternatively, would set off accessories in turquoise.

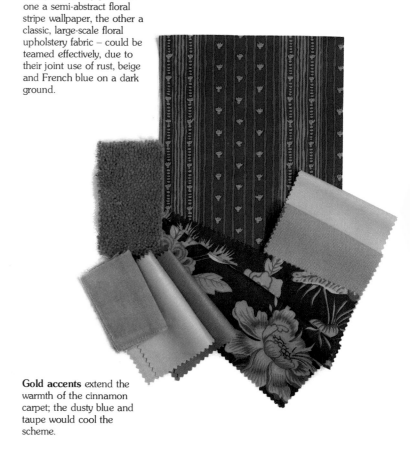

Gold accents extend the warmth of the cinnamon carpet; the dusty blue and taupe would cool the scheme.

The shimmering, moiré effect of light, medium and dark blue on an off-white ground is the room's most eye-catching pattern. It is made even more theatrical by the tented, alcove setting, heaped with large cushions.

The co-ordinating pastel stripes and checks of this textured wallpaper and glazed-cotton fabric contain several fresh, young colours suitable for accents and additional upholstery. Soft blue is ideal for carpeting.

Inject colour into the mainly achromatic scheme with furnishing fabrics of rich green, charcoal or gold: tones abstracted from the randomly patterned foil wallpaper.

The fabric's small-scale, repeating design – a stylized Egyptian scallop motif – neatly contrasts with both the random, textured screen-print on diamond-patterned, metallic foil and the soft, marbled 'book endpaper' print.

The carpet – checked with a narrow, double grid in navy enclosing a mid-blue, abstract leafy motif – expresses the colour scheme by way of the room's most rigid geometric pattern.

The room's mid-and deep-blues appear in the 'op-art' table-linen. This uses the busiest and densest of the patterns, one which is also the basis for the yellow and green accents.

FLORAL ABUNDANCE

A world without floral patterns is as unimaginable as a world without flowers, yet we can too easily take them for granted.

Look afresh at floral patterns. Flowers constitute the most widely used representational decorative motif. Their range is magnificent – from tiny, all-over spriggy prints to those containing gigantic, larger-than-life super-blooms.

Some look modern; some traditional; some sophisticated; some downright old-fashioned, and each has an ideal context in decorating. You can analyze them yourself according to line, colour and scale. Whether your scheme requires Eastern mystery, stately English propriety or a breezy Californian spirit, appropriate types of floral prints can do the trick.

If the idea of mixing floral patterns appeals, go for several rather than just one or two, and keep the colours compatible. If you are restricted to only a few, try for the same scale to create a further linking device.

Otherwise, indulge in a glorious crowd of prints for a heady, indoor garden of delight.

To achieve balance, it is usually easier to use a great many patterns rather than just two or three.

The exotic character of the room is increased by having a pattern on the ceiling rather than on the floor.

The tortoise-shell effect of the bamboo blind is evoked on a larger scale by the brushwork of the hand-painted shelves.

A sunny wallpaper with a spontaneous-looking floral motif, using light, chalky colours on a white ground, is ideal for a morning room or hallway. As it is a large-scale, random design, the types of patterns best suited to accompany it are small geometric ones in the soft blues, greens, apricots or yellows of the print. These colours could be used for carpet, curtains, upholstery or accent cushions. Green plants would look well against this paper and enhance its outdoor feeling; furniture painted white or yellow would suit the walls' happy, young character.

There is a natural link in this collection of Eastern prints: all use the same rich range of oranges, reds and deep purples.

Stripes are not out of place alongside paisley and floral prints as long as their colours are compatible.

The fabrics have patterns which are of a similar scale, but vary in their amount of white background.

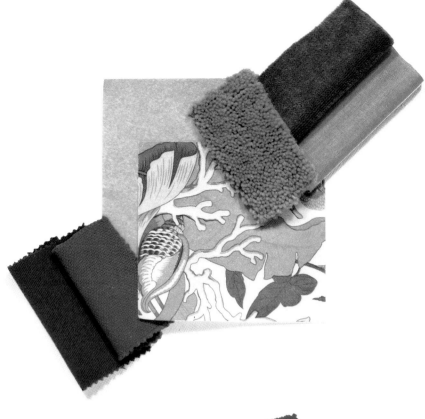

The neutral, beach-scape tones of this sophisticated wallpaper print can best be used on carpet and walls. The little geometric motif on the shell could be interpreted in upholstery or textured drapes. To maintain the cool, serene feel of the pattern, the various blues may be used in quantity elsewhere. To warm things up, do more with the deep coral outlining the various shapes. For a soft, romantic look, round out the scheme with the print's pastels and mid-tones; or add drama by emphasizing the stronger constituent colours.

A more mature image is suggested by this collection of fabrics and papers in shades of traditional dusty rose and jade-to-moss greens. Glazed chintz strikes the right balance between cosiness and formality. Teaming either floral print with dove-grey carpet would make an elegant scheme; using the green would give more of the comfort of the country.

The central abstract print, in varied strengths of pink on white, sounds a more modern note while retaining traditional coloration, which makes it compatible with the various florals.

The small-motif, tone-on-tone red wallpaper could be used with either the large- or small-pattern chintz; it is equally appropriate for use in a communicating passage or hallway.

CONQUERING SPACE

The true size and shape of a room are constant; but you can change the appearance of length, width and height by the way you use colour. Although a cubicle cannot be transformed into a ballroom, there are still countless decorating Cinderella stories in which colour acts as fairy godmother.

The most common problem area in these over-crowded times is how to make a little space go farther. There are, however, more subtle considerations: what to do with a long, narrow hallway, a low ceiling or too box-like a shape.

Evaluate a room in terms of the surfaces that give it its shape, and think of the contribution that each of them makes to the whole. Most of the time you are dealing with a basic set of six planes – four walls, a floor and a ceiling. The colours you apply to them can make each appear to advance or recede and to look larger or smaller in comparison to each other.

Strong colours have the effect of closing in. Red, orange and bright yellow literally jump out to meet the eye. They are 'advancing' colours: the effect arising from the fact that light at the red end of the spectrum focuses just behind the retina; while green settles relaxingly upon it, and the blues and violets come to a focus just in front of it to give the impression of receding.

Any dark colour will have a diminishing effect on area, which is why people are perennially admonished to wear black if they want to look slim. Thus, strength of tone is as important as hue. Although blue, for instance, is a receding colour, a room decorated entirely in dark blue will have the enclosed quality of a grotto, rather than the cool, drifting, boundless effect on an ethereal pastel blue.

Pale shades on the walls of a narrow room will appear to widen it; a pale ceiling will seem to lift away, and treading pale floorboards gives a subconscious feeling of walking on air. Dark paint will lower a high ceiling, but this effect must be handled judiciously – the use of a slightly deeper tone of wall paint can be sufficient; otherwise you risk creating a top-heavy, dark 'lid'. A strong colour on the floor will anchor the room and draw the eye down, and a plain shade is more space-enhancing than a pattern.

When all the surfaces have been decorated to produce the desired illusion, wave the magic wand of imaginative lighting to help complete the transformation.

A reddish brown seems to advance, emphasizing this low ceiling. Carried down to the bottom of the dividing beam, it unifies the rooms by camouflaging the division.

Dark objects are silhouetted against a light-coloured wall – the best way to appreciate the delicate tracery and enlivening green of plants.

White walls open the room out and emphasize its breadth. They reinforce its long, low look and strengthen the unifying role of the ceiling colour.

A light carpet completes the unification by colour of two functionally separate areas into a single space.

The stronger the overall colour of a room, the more closed in it feels. Here, deep khaki-brown walls and ceiling make the living room look smaller and cosier.

All-over white has the opposite effect, expanding the apparent volume of the dining alcove and making a separate room of it.

Light-coloured furnishings stand out in bold contrast against dark walls.

A light carpet restores an impression of spaciousness, and prevents the living-room from becoming too oppressively cave-like.

The white ceiling makes the living-room look higher – a device which works well only in a room as large as this. Dark walls and a very light ceiling could make a room as small as the dining alcove feel like an elevator.

The warm avocado green, used on all the walls and on the ceiling of the dining alcove, makes the alcove look as if it were simply an indentation in the wall. The white ceiling defines the living room and looks comparatively higher.

The ceiling and the rest of the walls of the living-room, as in the alcove, are in a single shade. The pale cream makes a cool, spacious contrast to the adjoining hot spot.

By alternating plum and white surfaces, living-room and dining alcove are simultaneously separated and unified. The total effect is to create an awareness of different planes and to produce an optical illusion that the small ceiling is cantilevered, supported by the larger expanse of the living-room wall.

Walls of different colours in the main room accord special emphasis to the alcove as its framing wall is painted a matching shade

Although the alcove has been given a deeper colour, the particular shade chosen has not made it claustrophobic; rather, this concentration of yellow in a small space is so charged with energy, it glows.

You and colour

Before you brandish a brush, take stock of the many details
which must be successfully integrated to attain a winning
scheme. Start by looking at yourself – at your true nature
and at the life you lead. Depending on whether you are a
night-owl or an early bird, an extrovert or a loner, your
colour choices may be rich or airy, stimulating or soothing.

Analyse your preferences room by room. Bedrooms can
be decorated to make you leap up with the new day or curl
up after the old. Living-rooms may be high-powered or
homey, but are invariably the most public part of your living
space. Eating areas are every bit as diverse as restaurants –
intimate or casual, formal or family – and are ideal settings
for occasional changes of colour. One-room living gives you
no place to hide, you must show your true colours; so go
ahead and flaunt them. Companionably cluttered or
ascetically sparse, warm or cool, low-profile or high-tech –
every approach has an appropriate colour angle.

Having worked out your personal priorities, see how they
can be meshed in with the salient characteristics of your
home: the pattern of natural light, the shape and
dimensions of the rooms, the climate and location. All of
these will have a bearing on the colour combinations you
choose. For inspiration, look at your favourite things. Any
collection – from Audubon prints to Zulu beadwork – can
be set off to advantage as the focal point of a completely
original scheme, tailored to reflect your interests. Even if
you are not a collector by nature, you will find certain things
– books or flower motifs – accumulate in nearly every
home, and they can be the basis for a singularly
comfortable theme. Once you appreciate your own, and
your home's, natural resources, you are ready to do
decorative justice to both.

From a postcard memory of a Greek island trip to a rainbow of papers and
pencils, inspiration is all around you.

ANALYSE YOURSELF

Before you start looking at the space you want to decorate, take a good look at yourself – not just in the mirror (although a knowledge of which colours flatter you is useful) but right inside. A successful colour scheme must integrate the needs of each room, according to structure and function, with your personal requirements.

Begin by asking such questions as: am I gregarious or self-contained? A night owl or a day bird? An extrovert or reserved? Do I want comfort or an impressive effect?

How much do I want to emphasize special interests, sports or hobbies? What do I hang on the walls – prints of old masters, original works, maps, photographs; are they abstract or representational; and do certain colours recur?

Do I generally prefer bare walls and clean surfaces, or find clutter companionable? Am I neat or disorderly? Do I seek serenity or stimulus?

Consider whether you get recreational pleasure out of decorating and enjoy changing schemes regularly, or whether you have a fixed idea about the ideal look for a room and simply freshen it periodically. Do you assimilate ideas from travel, friends and magazines, or do you look inside your own head and at your existing possessions for inspiration?

Do you entertain frequently or rarely, formally or informally? Are you interested in the impact your home has on others, or are you happy as long as it suits you? Do you prefer effects that are dramatic or almost subliminal?

The astrological sun signs are an amusing departure for such evaluations. These brief generalizations could not be expected to suit all, but let them be thought-provoking; even saying, 'I'm nothing like that!' is a first step towards the serious question, 'What am I really like?'

Aries 21 March–20 April *Fire* Diamond
Taurus 21 April–21 May *Earth* Sapphire
Gemini 22 May–21 June *Air* Agate
Cancer 22 June–22 July *Water* Pearl
Leo 23 July–23 August *Fire* Ruby
Virgo 24 August–22 September *Earth* Sardonyx
Libra 23 September–23 October *Air* Sapphire
Scorpio 24 October–22 November *Water* Opal
Sagittarius 23 November–21 December *Fire* Topaz
Capricorn 22 December–20 January *Earth* Turquoise
Aquarius 21 January–18 February *Air* Amethyst
Pisces 19 February–20 March *Water* Moonstone

Inventive, independent Aquarius, the water carrier, is an intellectual with a quirky flair. Interiors tend toward either of two extremes, uncluttered or cram-packed, depending on whether they require clear spaces in which to think, or live so deeply in the mind that disorder goes unnoticed. They have a penchant for ethnic furnishings, and their own original artwork.

Intuitive, impressionable Pisces, the fishes, is the dreamer. Interiors reflect the influence of others, although given a personal interpretation rather than left a direct copy. They prefer harmony to contrast, and feature items of sentimental value.

Headstrong, energetic Aries, the ram, spends so much time charging around in the outside world that home is a necessary sanctuary – the place to retreat and revitalize, often by bringing the outdoors in. Sociable Aries like schemes that encourage frequent casual entertaining, but are more concerned with pleasing themselves with their decorating than catering to others' tastes.

Humorous, practical Capricorn, the goat, is rarely house-proud, but does make steady improvements to the home, tending to ponder and experiment before leaping into big investments. They keep selected items of personal meaning, but do not hoard or cling to possessions.

Kindly, persistent Taurus, the bull, systematically acquires handsome possessions and derives great satisfaction from the home. Even urban Taureans cultivate rural fantasies, preferring wild-flower pastels to the hot-house brights.

Versatile, freedom-loving Sagittarius, the archer, will not be fenced in, and would rather live in one large room than a couple of small ones, but can adapt any area to enhance space. Artefacts from travel to exotic places predominate.

Passionate, resourceful Scorpio applies a private, intense personality and analytical mind to linking themes, subtly unifying the interior, and giving it an unmistakable, individual stamp. Bedrooms are especially atmospheric.

Idealistic, comfort-loving Libra, the scales, creates refined, tranquil schemes with a seemingly effortless colour balance. They may have trouble making up their minds about what they really want, but once they decide, they carry out the work with finesse.

Virgo, the discriminating perfectionist, often shares a home with cats, for they are similarly fastidious. Schemes that stay tidy and don't show the dirt – such as neutrals with exquisite accents – are favoured. Navy, chocolate and slate grey are indispensable. Virgo devotes particular attention to the bathroom, making it welcoming and civilized, rather than haphazard.

Imaginative, spontaneous Gemini, the twins, is attracted by anything new, and inherent restlessness inclines this sign to redecorate often, or to update existing schemes. Habitual hospitality makes the living/dining area a natural focus.

Artistic, home-loving Cancer, the crab, integrates style with domesticity. Elegant, but never aggressive, their schemes are harmonious and sensitive to the needs of others. When Cancers move, they excel at achieving a finished, lived-in look almost immediately.

Extravagant, extrovert Leo, the lion, is the flamboyant host. Leos are fanatical about their kitchens, and money is no object – not merely to make it look good but to ensure it performs perfectly. With no fear of being overpowered by their surroundings, Leos can opt enthusiastically for strong, contrasting schemes and will expect them to be admired. Sunny rooms, bursting with light, appeal most.

QUALITY OF RECEPTION

The living-room is invariably the most public part of the home; it is where family, friends and visitors gather, and where most entertaining is done. No matter how informal, it acts as a showcase. Consequently, the colours you use here have their greatest impact on others, influencing their mood as well as their impression of you.

If drama is your aim, familiarize yourself with a variety of this century's recurring themes: the jewel-bright, harem-tented look inspired by Diaghilev's touring Ballets Russes; the Art Deco reflection of black-and-white cinema glamour; the Seventies' nostalgia for rich, ornate Victoriana; the showy primaries and cool achromatics of high-tech, and the Eighties' reaction – a passion for pastels. If any of these examples of the theatrical-set approach to living-rooms appeals to you, use it as a possible way to go.

But if plain living takes precedence over a calculated image for formal entertaining, start right from scratch. Evaluate all the most basic of practical considerations.

The living-room is usually the largest room in the house, with the best natural lighting. Obviously starting points for schemes are such large investments as carpet, sofas, works of art or valued collections.

Think whether you use the room as much by day as by night. If keeping things clean is difficult for you, remember solid darks are as tricky as whites because they show specks; try patterns or neutrals. Evaluate your wardrobe and complexion, avoiding schemes in detracting tones.

Consider the living-room your stage, and be sure to colour it in such a way as to put the *real* you in the limelight.

The smoked-glass mirror, occupying an entire wall, is dramatic and paradoxical in effect. Although dark tones normally shrink a room, the mirror expands this one through a sophisticated veil of 'greige'.

The gleaming, marble-look table is made of wood, sprayed with grey dots and lacquered to resemble polished stone. It is a tonal link with the classical torso, and crucial to the neutral scheme.

The Italian-marble floor initiates a flow of white, spreading to walls, ceiling, curtains and upholstery. The resulting sea of light provides an impeccable, gallery-quality setting for the ancient sculpture.

Glossy black lacquer walls are the powerful context for a focal point, created by the ornately-framed modern masterpiece by Francis Bacon hanging above a fireplace of boldly patterned marble.

The smooth expanse of gold ceiling gives relief to the eye in a room so generously endowed with things to look at. Seen contrasted with the deep-lavender evening sky, the gold is a satisfying complementary, in keeping with the scheme's opulence.

Books do more than furnish a room; in this case they decorate it as well. Their bright spines contribute to the city-by-night coloration of a scheme which glows with cleverly-lit reds and ambers, like traffic signals and tail-lights, generating glamour.

Voluminous drapes, with theatrically large, soft tie-backs, give a seductive tented look and add a note of accent blue where they twist. The impression of restrained indulgence is reinforced by the enormous, pastel cushions heaped on the sofa.

Accessories in crystal and silver, from ultra-modern table sculpture to traditional candelabra, bring the elegance of a formally appointed dining-table into the living-room. Their achromatic surfaces reflect and transmit the room's delicate pastels.

Fine brass highlights, which extend to integral lamp-brackets, brilliantly accentuate the lines of the bookshelves and windows – framing as works of art both the colourful array of book bindings and the river view.

The rich, garnet-red and gold carpet, with its smart geometric patterning, underscores the consistent use of warm colours throughout the room, notably the honey-toned upholstery.

The white upholstery has an almost quilted look, important in a scheme where interesting textures augment quiet colours. A soft, neutral wool carpet is both opulent and quite practical.

Fragile tints of peach and dusty blue link the chic, sleek coffee-table with the luxuriously plump sofa cushions. The gentle colours mingle harmoniously in the peacefully hushed and low-lit atmosphere.

RETIRING TYPES

The bedroom is a place for constructive self-indulgence. Your scheme will be influenced by whether you are nocturnal or day-oriented; whether the room includes a desk, dressing-table or comfy reading-chair; whether you go there to switch off or just change gear; whether you fancy a romantic cocoon or a provocative parlour. Your lifestyle, as much as the room's physical attributes, will suggest suitable colours. Bedspreads are comparable to sofa covers in their thematic importance, but can be changed more easily. Had you ever longed for a pale carpet, this is the most practical setting – free from the worst tracked-in dirt and household spills. All the rooms shown here, despite widely differing styles, have opted for a lighter shade of pile.

The whites-and-brights room – with unlimited potential for seasonal changes – is energizing to wake up in, and perhaps to catch up with correspondence over coffee; the pastel scheme is a soothing antidote to city stress with its tranquil, homespun chic; the lair-look is unabashedly seductive, revelling in tactile textures and the intimacy evoked by dark schemes.

Your own bedroom is your sanctuary, so colour it to satisfy your soul.

Filmy curtains, a draped table, ribbon-ties on the lampshades and vases of cut flowers balance and romanticize a scheme, weighted towards breezy efficiency.

The unusual tile-pattern wall covering gives these surfaces a graphic strength far superior to plain white paint, but as cleanly in appearance.

The framed museum poster is the ingenious key to the scheme, combining both the bedspread motif of bright spots and the grid pattern, echoed on the wall.

The multicolour-stippled bedspread cheerfully dominates an otherwise largely neutral room. All accessory colours may be traced to its print.

A soft, suede-look beige 'skin' covers the floor – a pleasing textural foil to the many hard-edged features and, like all the permanent fixtures, a light neutral.

Accessories – lamp, vases, picture frames – with smooth, clean lines and pale colours add visual interest by way of the personal touch, while keeping the look light and uncluttered.

A chevron-patterned, pastel bedspread, hand-crafted from old shirting fabrics, sets the room's mellow, relaxing colour mood, with a blend of chalky blues and peachy, ice-cream shades. Pillowcases have been dyed to match.

Delicate apricot paint on the sloping wall, with deeper-toned window trim, has a warming, civilizing effect on this thoughtfully converted attic room.

The ornately-framed mirror, massive and dark, sets the tone for the furnishings: mahogany chests of drawers, brown leather bedstead – all rich and heavy in character – so the room has a grand atmosphere, even though, as the mirror reveals, it is not particularly large.

Where furs and skins are the medium, sensuality and luxury are the message. Here an extravagant throw of real fur from a cold climate is complemented by plush cushions, whose prints are bold fakes of exotic beasts from the tropics.

White carpet, in the context of an otherwise consciously dark setting, is a dramatic and glamorous touch. It also points up the whites in the pillow and bed-cover prints.

Lacquered wicker panels on the wall reflect the low light and accentuate the jungle look. The baskets and lampshade repeat the texture in varied neutrals.

TABLE SETTING

Eating areas can reflect life-styles more than any other part of the home. What, where, when and with whom you eat are highly revealing, and provide perfect starting points for your colour scheme. Settings range from casual, eat-in kitchens to formal dining-rooms, from breakfast-bars to barbecues.

No matter how informal, eating is usually a social experience; a good colour scheme will enhance it. Restaurateurs favour red because of its stimulating effect on appetite and conversation, but it could be overpowering in the home. The dining atmosphere is built up more from decorative detail than from broad canvasses of colour. Although the table assumes an importance comparable to that of the sofa in the living-room or the bed in the bedroom, its appearance is far more variable – usually a neutral with an array of accessories changing with the season and the occasion: from party-time paper plates and napkins to good crystal, china and damask.

Often the eating area is an outgrowth or integral part of either the living-room or the kitchen, or it is part of a sequence linking the two; this may influence your choice of colour.

Evolve your scheme with regard to how much you entertain, your funiture style, the effects of low lighting, key colours in your china – even your food preferences – light for fresh salads; warm for rich, hot dishes – and season to taste. *Bon appétit!*

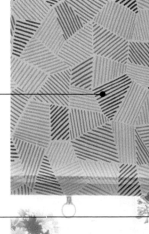

A crazy quilt-pattern of stripes in primaries and secondaries enlivens the blind with real graphic punch and – with colours repeated in the toys below – accentuates the youthful atmosphere of the room.

Immaculate white tile bounces the light off its shiny surface, giving the room a neat, workmanlike appearance. It is possible, with this permanent backdrop, to devise endless future colour stories, simply by changing the variables – blind, chair paint, lampshade – that determine the current scheme's focus.

The hard-wearing, dark blue floor makes a crisp colour contrast to the white kitchen units and appliances, but is hardly more practical than a light floor in houskeeping terms, for its solid finish will show up specks and spills.

The two-tone wall treatment – apricot and parchment – has lightened the room nicely and reconciled the period furniture with modern art in a way that traditional flocked wallpaper could not have done.

The rich wood furniture establishes the room's formal elegance, ideally suiting its proportions. Accents of cherry red in the upholstery, lamp glass and paintings echo the wood's own natural, warm highlights.

White carpet, a technical extravagance in a dining-room, contrasts dramatically with the dark mantelpiece, highlights the white gloss trim and brightens the overall atmosphere, unlike the expected wood floors and coloured rugs.

The pale, pinky-beige trim on the cream units adds a stylish, tailored note – a reminder that the kitchen may not be given over permanently or completely to the young, but could readily be modified for a more sophisticated effect.

Cream-coloured cabinetwork and kitchen units, a range of white accessories and the expanse of white table combine to make the room appear airy, light and spacious.

The party goods are a touch of temporary colour, thoughtfully selected to blend harmoniously with the rest of the room. Their stripe motif is a pleasing echo of the window blind, and the bold primaries are incorporated instantly into the larger colour focus of chairs and lampshade.

The gaily painted chairs are the focal point of the room, each one a fun variation on the theme of cheerful primaries. Their mood is fresh, happy, young, energetic and completely informal.

CLOSE QUARTERS

One-room living presents a considerable decorating challenge, but start from one unequivocal point: this scheme must, above all, suit you – your own comfort and convenience. It can still have a positive impact on others – it is bound to, in that it concentrates self-expression – and few home-making skills are more impressive than the ingenious adaptation of confined quarters, where intimacy is a fact of life.

When you must live, sleep and perhaps even work in the same room, you face a special problem, namely, the claustrophobic sensation that you have no immediate alternative. The rooms shown illustrate two diametrically opposed solutions.

The white studio represents a classic approach to maximizing the appearance of space, for white is known to make any surface look larger. It also acknowledges the paramount need a working artist has for light. The pink and blue theme gives it variety, but keeps it airy, so that the abundant white is not too clinically severe. The complete design, with its hushed, blanched interpretation of basic red, white and blue, indicates a preference for serenity.

The opposite is true of the exuberant, one-room 'bazaar'. Here the use of colour is stimulating and uninhibited – an aggregate effect calculated to bedazzle. However, one could not sensibly work in this environment, where the eye is perpetually distracted. It is a magpie's dream.

Between these two extremes is a vast range of one-room styles – plant-packed indoor gardens, contrasting shades defining functional areas, monochromatic mood-making – to suit L-shapes, alcoves, loft beds, or any living space which exhibits the open-plan principle in microcosm. The amount of time you spend in these surroundings will affect your colour choices and may persuade you to change regularly. At least, begin with those you would want as room-mates.

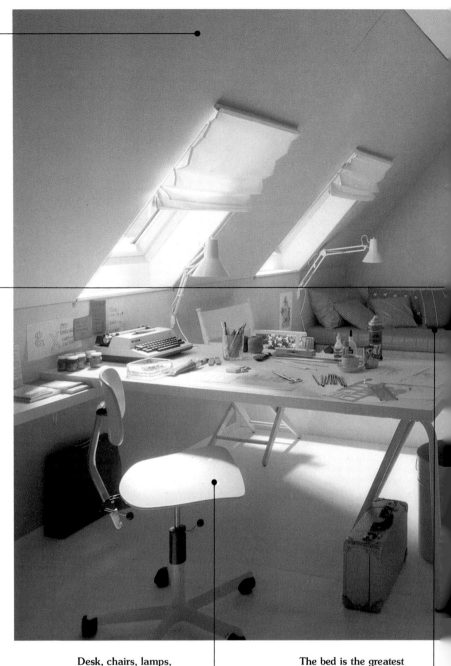

Stark, arctic white walls, floors and woodwork create a wraparound effect, converting this small attic room into an energizing capsule of light. With no natural wood visible, there is an artificial, rather futuristic effect. The implication is that white was chosen to maximize the sense of space and order.

Many small touches around the room – the poster, the dried flowers, the blue lampshade, the notices behind the typewriter – develop the pink-and-blue accent theme.

Desk, chairs, lamps, blinds, round storage bin, even television, were chosen deliberately to keep the room – and the work area in particular – as uniformly white as possible. Normally these variables, technically separate from the permanent shell of the room, would be obvious subjects for colour contrast.

The bed is the greatest focus of colour in the room: two neatly stacked bricks of china blue and chalky pink, which match each other perfectly in value and intensity, with a glazed finish to reflect the light. The collection of pillows on top expands the colour theme – the heart-shaped one a grace feminine note.

Colours and images crowd the walls in an uninhibited collage, which, for all its apparent madness, on close inspection reveals a method. Background panels of brilliant lacquer red, cellophane yellow and magenta impose a discreet order. Diaphanous fabrics and ethnic embroideries enrich the composition.

A floral theme runs riot on the bed. A group of related cushions help to melt it into the wall collage, camouflaging the extent to which it dominates the room. The red bedspread is the warm centre from which the kaleidoscopic decoration radiates. Bold, bright floor cushions denote a lounging, or casual eating, area.

A stack of cushions in blue and white – stripes, checks and florals – forms a visual link with those on the bed, and can be deployed for extra seating along the edge of the platform. To complete the picture, even the pet's bed has blue cushions.

Yellow-painted floorboards complete the impression that no surface has been left undecorated. Bright, Easter-egg colours have also been used to treat the door moulding like a picture frame, and to dress up the bedside chest of drawers.

Collecting and collections are the inspiration for this amiably cluttered fantasy-land. The objects and images are whimsical, gem-bright and often brazenly kitsch. The five large white ceramic pieces stand out like beacons in the chaotic colourscape. A stack of hats atop a painted bust evokes their zany owner.

71

ANALYSE YOUR SITUATION

When you have taken account of your personal needs and preferences, have a good look at the physical attributes of your living space. These include natural lighting, climate and location, as well as the actual size and shape of rooms. Colour can work for you even when Nature and architecture go against you; and, of course, it can make the most of your home's blessings.

First observe how the sunlight tracks around your house. Although the sun's daily movement from east to west – and the direction each room faces – remains constant, the amount of light they get differs with the seasons. A sun-facing room with negligible window area, or with tall buildings towering over it, may be no lighter than one with vast picture windows, or skylights, which is poorly angled toward the sun. Walls containing windows will appear darker than walls on which the light falls, so you could choose to make them lighter. Warmer or lighter colours are usually prescribed for chilly or darkish rooms, but you can interpret these ground rules according to how the room is to be used.

Climate is a psychological and cultural influence, as well as physical factor in colour choice. For instance, the constant brilliant sunshine about which the fogbound fantasize can, in reality, be fatiguing. The correct cool colours can create a balance without contradicting the character of the setting.

The surroundings of your home can affect the treatment of the interior – either as a cocoon, safely separate from outside blight, or an integral showcase for a lovely garden or view.

Moving inside, check the dimensions of the rooms. Are they bigger or smaller than you would like? Are any of them awkward shapes? Evaluate ceiling height, wall space, storage areas, door openings and what they reveal; picture likely traffic patterns, and estimate the amount of time you expect to spend in any given room at any given time of day.

When you have studied the anatomy of your home and the kind of life you intend to lead in it, make up scale floorplans as we have done here. People normally make such drawings to test arrangements of furniture, but if you take it a step further and add colour, you will get an invaluable insight into your proposed scheme. Colour is too important to be an afterthought; planning ahead is a practical pleasure.

This studio apartment in a cold climate gets plenty of direct natural light during the day, but not in the evening when its working owner needs it most. The living area and kitchen are painted red for warmth, drama and unity. White woodwork, floor tiles and pale carpet are a second linking theme. Green plants bring the scheme alive.

evening light

Black for the bathroom is an effective foil for the red used elsewhere. White floor and fittings, as well as mirror walls, enhance space.

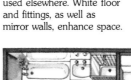

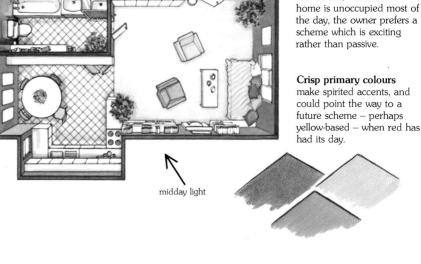

midday light

morning light

Red is a bold choice for a wall colour, but since this home is unoccupied most of the day, the owner prefers a scheme which is exciting rather than passive.

Crisp primary colours make spirited accents, and could point the way to a future scheme – perhaps yellow-based – when red has had its day.

This one-bedroomed townhouse apartment receives most daylight through the bay window of the living-room; its brightness is further magnified by off-white walls and a cream carpet. The latter has been used throughout as a linking device, except in the kitchen where more practical cork tiles have been installed.

Warm, related shades – a glowing mustard and a rich brown – have been chosen for bedroom and bathroom. The latter has a mirror wall, maximizing light and space.

The kitchen catches a useful amount of natural light passed on from the living-room. It is painted a matching shade of off-white, illuminating the work area.

morning light

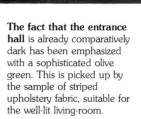

The outside wall has been painted white to reflect as much daylight as possible into the bedroom window, overlooking the little courtyard. The bedroom naturally captures the best of the evening light.

evening light

The fact that the entrance hall is already comparatively dark has been emphasized with a sophisticated olive green. This is picked up by the sample of striped upholstery fabric, suitable for the well-lit living-room.

midday light

This split-level, suburban family house in a temperate climate has great scope and versatility. The three main areas – lower-level family rooms, passageway and children's rooms, and parents' bedroom suite – are distinguished by their unifying floor treatments.

Deeper, warmer shades – tawny-golds and wine-reds – were chosen for the living-room and dining-room, facing away from the sun and used mostly in the evenings. The small entrance hall is painted wraparound red for a warm welcome.

The sun sweeps in an arc from one end of the swimming pool to the other, with the deck-chairs gleaning the evening rays. The pool-facing rooms, which catch both the sun and its reflection from the water most of the day – and hence tend to heat up – are in light, clear citrusy colours, to echo the garden's freshness.

The living-room, dining-room and entrance hall have in common a polished wood floor, neutral in tone, and suited to any colour scheme. Here it is enlivened with handsome area rugs. Stone tiles are practical for the kitchen and family room.

These agreeable pastels are sample tones for accessories, or even large-scale redecoration of the master-bedroom suite, and are compatible with the fitted apricot carpet.

The children's rooms make up for the somewhat utilitarian blue/grey carpet with a lively scheme of whites, yellows and blues, accented with the other primary colour, red. The blue stripe sample is a suggestion for curtains or bedspreads.

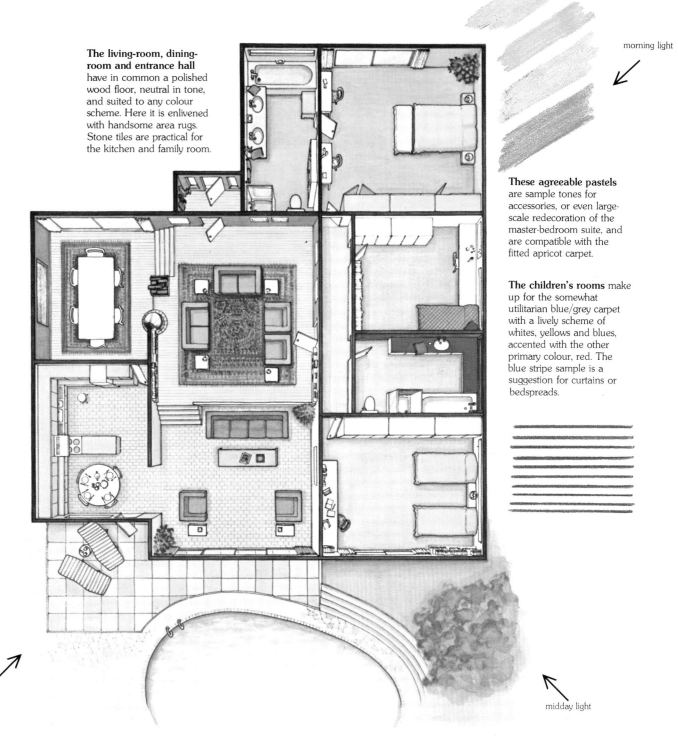

morning light

midday light

evening light

PERSONAL PROMPTS

A few of your favourite things ... what better way to begin a colour scheme? No matter what you collect – African masks to mechanical toys, seashells to ceramics – you will be confronted with a fascinating range of tints and shades around which you can build a dramatic, original scheme. Whether valued for investment or sentiment, your prized possessions will be displayed to best advantage, and your choice of colours will reflect the real you, as seen in the things you love.

Often colour is a key factor, attracting you to the things you collect, in the first place. If you extend their characteristic tones around the room, it will enhance your delight in them. Start simply by studying them. Note the main colours and the proportions in which they occur; then think which would be suitable for specific surfaces. If you keep the links subtle, they will have greater staying power, for the connections gradually, gratifyingly, bloom in the eye.

Think of the different, personally designed backdrops you could create, using such colour crafts as collage, stencil, marbling or stippling, which would enable you to combine the colours, textures and even images ideal for your collection.

At the same time as you are evaluating colour, consider texture; it can have a deciding influence over the way a chosen colour 'feels' and actually appears. You need to surround your collection with textures that are compatible, or that constitute a satisfying foil.

Have fun with this approach. If you have, say, a hoard of beach-combing booty – shells, pebbles, water-weathered glass – why not a pale, perhaps flecked, carpet; walls either sea or sky blue, or one of the delicate, sun-bleached pinks, greys or off-whites which could also be used for curtains or upholstery, possibly with a shell motif?

A particular pleasure of collecting is the way in which the whole seems more magical than the sum of its parts; you can extend this enjoyment to your colour scheme.

This glass collection – ranged light to dark, clear to green – is as subtly tinted as it is fragile. It is displayed to advantage against cream-painted walls, with sympathetically toned pen drawings in matching cream mounts and polished aluminium frames. The fine, open-wire mesh shelving enhances the play of light around and through the collection. An exquisite unifying touch is the glass bowl containing cream-coloured pebbles and bulbs with delicate green shoots.

Any one of these hand-wrought wooden objects would be appealing to look at on its own, but seen together they are richer, more satisfying and more intriguing. Their smooth, softly glowing surfaces reveal the mellow spectrum of natural wood colours, from golden to red chestnut to brownish-black. They create a splendid geometric sampler of stripes, squares and diamonds – inspirations for decorating motifs.

Although the glass and metal objects are old, a scheme built around them could feature modern furniture, while celebrating gleam and transparency in a tranquil setting devoid of any overpowering colour.

Emphasis on warm neutrals and natural textures – ethnic rugs, polished wood floors, hand-woven blankets, raw-linen upholstery, bamboo, wicker and masses of plant greenery – would be the most flattering setting.

The background painting is a major asset in a scheme built around the majolica collection because it uses related coloration, albeit in somewhat dustier, matt tones. Similarly primitive figures add to the unity.

These quaint majolica figures are a treasure-trove of unusual colours – musty green and squash-blossom yellow-orange, with mauve-blue accents – the basis for a scheme of real originality and vitality.

The flowers have been hand-picked to match the key glaze tones and the simple shapes of the blooms shown in relief on the pots. They justify the use of suitably coloured floral patterns on soft furnishings.

COVER STORIES

It is a truism that 'books do furnish a room,' but they have even more to offer than friendly integrity and intimacy. Almost everyone has a book collection of some description, but it is often scattered about on any shelf space that will hold it, with no thought for its decorative potential.

Of all our possessions, books are the most sensitive mirror of personality; no other collection is so multi-faceted.

Few other collections are so multicoloured, either. Since we don't buy books according to their colour, how can we sensibly use them as a basis for decoration?

Three different approaches are shown here: the first is a working library, humanized with bric-à-brac and colour-coded in accordance with the owner's obvious interest in Art Nouveau; the second treats the books as a work of art, framing them charmingly in a specially constructed case, and setting them off with carefully ordered arrangements of related objects, above and below, in colours reflecting the warm tones of the books' spines. The third over-

rides their individual identities so that they become an abstract blur – set-dressing in a consciously elegant room which has been decorated as if it were an expensively-bound, gold-leaf edition.

In devising your own scheme, consider whether there are categories into which large numbers of your books fall which evoke certain colours – such as celadon for China; achromatics for film history or Art Deco; vivid, velvety greens, blues and henna-reds for Pre-Raphaelite painting.

Decide whether you want your books dressed up or down, formal or casual; if they are to be used, or admired from afar; whether they should leap to the eye from a light background or be snuggled into a dark one. You can arrange books in coherent colour groups, but our perception of books, our conditioned response to them, regardless of how jumbled, is that they never seem to clash, any more than flowers do. Adjust the colours according to the needs of the room; books are equally at home in living-rooms, bedrooms and studies. Refer to them when you want your interior to turn over a new leaf.

The books are presented as a work of art, framed in tortoise-shell against a golden glowing wall: the case specially built to house them, the table virtually banked with tribute to their subjects.

Art Nouveau patterned wallpaper in characteristic peacock blue and green, forms a frieze, above and below shelves painted a matching turquoise. A pair of china peacock book-ends reinforces the Art Nouveau theme.

Occasional volumes turned face-out, as in a bookstore display, become integral graphic works or portraits, and underscore their owner's interest in Art Nouveau and biography. The accessible open shelves and nearby desk show that this is a working library, but one which has been beautified with assorted ceramic pieces, such as the vase on the top shelf, unifying the book colours with the blue wall.

The books have been grouped, in some cases, according to the colours of their spines, producing attractive blocks of yellow, red, blue, black and, midway down on the left, a matching set has been arranged rainbow-fashion.

A row of alternating busts and teapots, repeating the constituent colours of the tortoise-shelling, gives the scheme solidity and rhythm, while tacitly stating the grandly Bohemian theme of classics and collectables.

Inaccessibility relegates these books to the role of wallpaper. They create an abstract, almost geometric background, uninsistently multicoloured, over which hangs the modern art which here gets priority.

The black and gold framework evokes the feeling that the entire room has been bound as if it were a rare book. Classical details, such as the Greek key-motif curtains and slender black columns, create formality.

Rich tortoise-shelling, in a style reminiscent of book endpapers, embellishes the front of the bookcase and is repeated on the moulding above – an indication of the importance the bookcase has been given in this room.

The pale carpet and silk upholstery create a dramatic island of light, in the context of the rich, dark, book-lined walls, to which the furniture is linked by the gilt and the print's gold trellis motif.

The handsome composition of antiques and plants symmetrically assembled on the table derives both its eclectic content and its variegated coloration from the books featuring history and the decorative arts.

FLOWERS ALL THE WAY

Real and representational flowers are easily the most pervasive decorating motif in history. Recourse to Nature's beauty in such a concentrated, accessible form is universal.

Most homes already contain a variety of floral elements – vases of cut flowers; wallpaper, curtain or upholstery patterns; rugs or bedspreads; framed prints or paintings; pretty china – but their use is often random. It is possible to devise original schemes around flowers, developing the colours, textures and shapes systematically to achieve various specific effects.

You may draw inspiration from flowers in any of the three contexts shown – as art; as their ornamental selves; and as a printed design. A flower-based scheme need not be fussy, as the interior below reveals.

In any room, flowers remain an ideal source of instant – and readily changeable colour.

The quartet of Warhol paintings provides the colour cue for the entire scheme. Apart from their intrinsic value as art, they are an object lesson in the way colours affect dimension (compare the apparent sizes of identically shaped blooms) and the way they affect one another (the pungent complementaries versus the drifting pastels). Together they make a riveting focal point in an otherwise deliberately serene setting.

The luscious shade of solid peach, derived from a bloom in the upper-left painting, is the basis of a scheme harmoniously blending walls, upholstery, chair seats and even the low coffee table.

The carpet contributes greatly to the room's light atmosphere. Its trellis pattern, echoing the panel between window and door, is in the unifying peach shade used throughout.

The purply shade is picked up around the room in such touches as the branch coral, the African violets and the cushions on the sofa which also share the pictures' square format.

Tiny, Christmas-tree lights have been strung through this veritable flower 'shrine' to create a magical, twinkly effect at night – more imaginative than a single spotlight.

Sunlight streams through the stained-glass roundel in the window, setting its vibrant primary colours aglow. The timelessness of simple floral designs is expressed in the medieval-style inner border. The curtain has a similar, concentric motif.

Flowers in whatever quantity – even a solitary, long-stemmed rose – enhance a room; but this bravura display bombards the eye with all the colour-power that massed, mixed floral media can muster. It gaily combines growing flowers, cut flowers, dried flowers, high-quality artificial silk flowers and even plastic flowers, to show that in the right context, nothing succeeds like excess. This urban basement is blooming proof.

A decorative fringe benefit to this multitudinous assortment of bouquets is the variety of vases and *cache-pots* used as containers. The textures of their materials – glass, china, terracotta, wicker – and their colours – warm neutrals and whites – are useful foils, giving the composition balance and a lively, market feeling.

Flowers are raised in relief on these unusual bottles – a welcome element of clarity and light in such a densely coloured arrangement; yet still true to the overall floral theme.

The strongest bolt of colour in this otherwise all-pastel scheme comes from the vases of real flowers. Their glossy dark foliage stands out crisply in the soft, warm amber-lit setting. The eye-catching top table-cloth, with its graceful cut-out and silk-stitched border, features the shape, as much as the colour, of flowers. It introduces a three-dimensional quality to the decoration, as do the appliquéd and embroidered cushions on chair and sofa. Even the vases have a raised or applied floral motif.

Their related pastel shades make floral patterns of widely varying scales and motifs compatible. Most prominent is the medium-scale, coral-and-jade toned print of geometrically stylized morning glories and daisies, used on the sofa and matching curtains. The two table-cloths directly juxtapose the largest- and smallest-scale of the print patterns.

CANVASSING FOR IDEAS

The relationship of art to decorating should be unequivocal; the room accommodates the artwork, not vice versa, and the artwork accommodates the individual. Tamper with those priorities and dubious taste has got a foot in the door. Art is for life's sake, to respond to and to enjoy. As its appeal is intensely personal, it can also be the linchpin of a uniquely satisfying and original scheme.

When you find a painting you really love, your own creative contribution is to provide it with an organically related, supportive setting.

Study the piece you want to feature for colour, content, line and mood. In selecting your background and accents, take care not to suffocate the painting with too contrived a scheme. The rooms shown are strikingly monochromatic, giving the paintings plenty of breathing space. Furniture has been chosen to flatter the spirit of the artwork. Combine ingenuity with restraint for an interior that is truly a masterpiece.

The David Hockney painting is the jumping-off point for the entire scheme. It is the source of both the milder yellow on walls and ceiling, and the sharp, diving-board shade of the carpet. Seen in contrast to so much surrounding yellow, the blue strongly invites the eye. Like the painting, the room is hypnotically stilled by flat verticals and horizontals – relieved here with a bigger splash, there with a spray of lilies.

Light floods this room as if the sun were shining indoors. Two large, unadorned windows form bleached canvasses, echoing the painting's square format. From the ceiling track hang two large, theatrical spotlights, appropriate to the modern scheme in general and the painting's Hollywood theme in particular.

The wraparound white of walls, woodwork and glossy-painted floor reflects the abundant natural light from large windows, and charges the room with the painting's lively spirit. The globe lamp is irresistibly appropriate to the painting's main motif.

This painting galvanizes the interior with its 'atomic' energy. Scarlet 'electrons' appear about to whirl into the room, while a starry aperture draws the eye into the distance. The red circles and blue squares are the most intense colours anywhere in the scheme, leaving the painting the undisputed focal point.

Custom-built furniture flatters the painting with its square, clean lines, and colours that underscore rather than upstage. The sofa incorporates the many shades of pink used in the painting, and the 'points-up' arrangement of the pillows there and on the bed is a fittingly dynamic touch.

The crisply striped sofa upholstery plays off the blue and traces of brown in the painting, to which it relates in a sympathetically summery manner. Care has been taken to ensure that none of the furniture conflicts or competes – neutral brown sofa and cane-seated chairs, the latter another sub-tropical touch.

Vibrant colours, evoking African textiles and challenging optical tricks, make this large, geometric painting an unusual choice for the bedroom. The single canvas has the *effect* of twin panels, and this doubling motif has been repeated in the pillows, with their toning stripes, and in the two African carved wood stools.

Radiant yellow, the happiest colour in the spectrum, has been applied in a seamless flow around the room, assimilating all architectural detail. Such pronounced decorative homage to the painting has expanded its sunny spirit. Given the reputed powers of mental stimulus of both yellow and blue, this would also make a good work environment.

A panel of mirror squares is almost camouflaged by the sheer universality of yellow, nevertheless, it gives the room the added depth and visual interest of reflection. Additional glitter is supplied by the metal table and chair legs and the shade of the desk lamp.

A perfectly plain cocoa brown is the discreet neutral setting for the room's dramatic colour use. Paradoxically, while this earthy shade exerts a warm, intimate influence, the vast multiple mirrors flirt with the illusion of infinity.

The bedspread continues the colour story, while relieving the room of too rigid a symmetry. A random pattern, with the serpentine vitality and grace of vines, makes use of the pungent, moody vermilions, acid yellows, turquoises, stormy blues and red-violets of the painting. It is a work of art in its own right, made to order to unify this sophisticated scheme.

Putting colour to work

In decorating, colour is not just a pretty face; it is both a power tool and a precision instrument, ready to perform important practical tasks anywhere in the home.

When you require an immediate transformation, paint is the magic medium; for speed, economy and range of shades it has no equal. You can feel the excitement of colour in action with the first sweep of a freshly loaded roller over a dingy wall. Use it both to personalize new premises in a hurry, or to test colours for long-term schemes before investing in expensive, permanent items.

Once you have established your basic schemes, you can build a repertoire on a few key themes in the same way as you might develop your wardrobe. With walls and fixed furnishings as constants, you can treat such things as loose covers, curtains, table-, bed- and bath-linen, rugs, and other accessories – from ashtrays to cut flowers – as variables.

You can heighten your enjoyment of special occasions, vacation homes, or even picnics, with well-planned colour – the drama of a temporary, monochromatic scheme, or just the fun of decoration coordinated with your clothes.

On a more regular basis, you can, and should, orchestrate colour to provide the mood you want in each room, be it calming, practical or stimulating. Rooms, like faces, can be analyzed in terms of the focal points which are their features and the architectural qualities which, like bone structure, can be emphasized with colour highlights. At the same time, colour can define functional areas, coding them for work, relaxation, or other activities.

Finally, a well-thought-out scheme can unify any interior, relating the various rooms to one another in a natural progression, with colour creating the necessary visual links. The more ways you put colour to work, the better your home will work for you.

A great wall of china, the cream of the author's ceramic collection, parades across his larder, demonstrating colour at work in the kitchen.

QUICK BUT SLICK

There are always factors other than the purely aesthetic to be considered in decorating – namely time, energy and money.

When, for whatever reason, your efforts are to be of temporary benefit to you, you must consider how to get the most from a modest investment. If you live in a short-lease rented property or know you will soon be leaving, or if you have just moved into a place that is either downright dingy or decorated in a style that is to you hopelessly inimical, use colour to achieve a fast transformation with a finished look.

Paint, glorious paint, is your greatest ally. It can transform your surroundings in hours, and, moreover, do it more cheaply than any other medium.

When out to achieve an instant interior, one employs changes not requiring structural work, costly fixed furnishings – such as fitted carpet – or too much hard work. For instance, all three of the rooms shown here have painted floors: they won't stay dazzling forever without maintenance, but they do look superb in the short term (and there are now on the market excellent, durable paints specifically for use on floors). After all, not every wooden floor is a piece of master craftsmanship worthy of laborious sanding and varnishing.

So if your goal is top style at top speed, grab your brushes and rollers. Nothing is as fresh as paint.

A naked bulb symbolizes the desolate feeling of a new home, but, massed in this way, they create an amusing effect with raw impact. The lights shown have been wired separately, but several could be brought down from the same socket and pinned to hang this way or like a 'high-tech chandelier'.

The pink-painted folding chair sings a cheeky solo, its brilliance of hue and gloss setting it apart from its matt surroundings.

A 'trompe-l'oeil' painting of a ladder highlights the buoyant idiosyncrasy of this scheme, which has deliberately chosen to play up the unfinished look. If short of storage space during decorating, one could simply paint working ladders pink and prop them against a wall.

You're in the pink the moment you step through the door. Hallways are an ideal place to experiment with unusual colours as they are generally small areas, quick to paint, and one tends to pass quickly through rather than linger.

The painted floor reinforces the theme in a slightly deeper tone. Paint is the fastest, most economical route to a fresh floor finish.

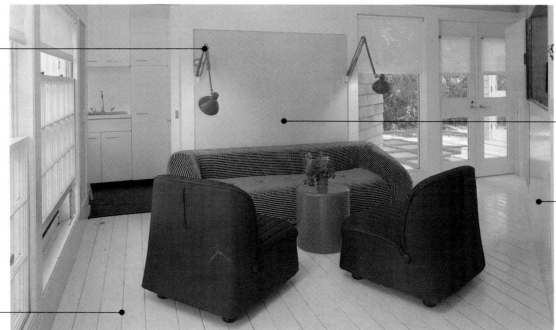

The primary red accents give indispensable vitality to this otherwise achromatic scheme. Notice how the triangular arrangement of the matching anglepoise lamps and drum table echoes the positioning of the two chairs and sofa. It is this almost subliminal symmetry which galvanizes the room, showing how a keen eye can devise an instant interior of real integrity.

A white floor, forever modern, forever fresh, does its share to fill the room with reflected light.

The grey-painted panel affords a visual respite from the all-pervasive white and, in turn, makes the white, by contrast, appear extra-clean.

Walls painted white – no start is fresher and no paint is cheaper. Here they accentuate the abundant natural light with which this room is blessed. White blinds complete the unified overall effect.

Indoor greenery is the perfect antidote to urban grime and grimness – a sparkling sanctuary filled with an exuberant assortment of foliage. Plants sit on the floor, hang from the ceiling, occupy spare space on shelves or ledges. The very air feels green. Yet for all its tranquillity, this is a highly movable feast for the eyes. The plants could be bought and installed in an hour. Growing things give the finishing touch that brings a room alive.

The rattan furniture keeps the mood light and fits in well with the tropical feel of the room. It is handsome, still comparatively inexpensive, readily available, and easy to transport and install. Wicker baskets for the plant pots complement the table and chairs, and all of these neutral items, including the terracotta pots, have the benefit of working well with any future scheme.

The loose sofa covers could be cheap canvas – or linen; such is white's charisma, they strike a luxurious note in an inexpensive room.

The white walls and floor are not merely expedient. They contribute to the conservatory atmosphere, amplifying the already generous supply of light from the large windows. They also make possible the subtle pleasure, in this plant-lover's paradise, of admiring the varied silhouettes of the individual leaf formations, which would otherwise be difficult to distinguish against a darker ground.

MAKING DO IN STYLE

Few people can afford to carry out a grand, master-plan design all in one go, and frequently an interior may not warrant much expenditure because you know your days there are numbered. Nevertheless, even in these circumstances, a judicious use of colour can still give complete-looking interior schemes. As in the creation of instant interiors, paint – instant colour – is the miracle worker. However, an increased use of accessories and fabric bring personality and unity to such a room.

The degree of commitment varies. If you are renting a furnished house or apartment, you might prefer to cover an unsightly table or chair with a handsome cloth that can be taken away with you when you go, rather than invest in laborious refinishing or reupholstering. Take advantage of short stays and interim schemes by trying out combinations of colours you are curious about, for possible use on a more permanent basis.

If tackling the decoration of a permanent home from bare boards, adding expensive items slowly, let low-priced accessories such as prints or cushions in key shades maintain a finished look at every stage. In such situations experimentation and expedience work together to give organic development.

Deep purple walls are provocatively moody. Their night-life shade is suited to someone who chooses to express a strong personality.

The lavender influence pervades the accessories; from the selection of fashion magazine tear-sheets and the glossy mirror frame to the clusters of hydrangea.

The small chest of drawers is the type of piece commonly found in furnished apartments, or picked up cheaply second-hand. Its intrinsic merit is negligible, so it is a ready candidate for decoration. Painting the drawer fronts in deliberately contrasted colours gives a touch of glamour to a humble necessity, and makes the chest a focal point for the room as a whole.

The fuschia-pink bedspread is an inspired foil both to the dark walls and the ornamental black pillows. As a solid, it contributes the precious illusion of space in confined quarters.

The vertical-striped motif adds a valuable extra dimension. It is expressed most clearly in the blinds and matching sofa cushion, but it also cleverly links the old-fashioned radiator to the rest of the interior.

The heavy-gauge wire shelves are overtly industrial – a note of high-tech. Because they are both neutral and free-standing, they can be moved anywhere for many uses.

The fabric draped over the sofa may be just a protective covering to keep pale upholstery clean during a party or a visit by children or animals. It might, however, be an expedient means of camouflaging a disreputable old hulk or inappropriate upholstery. Meanwhile it allows the trial of a strong colour in the room – which, if successful, could lead to a serious investment in red.

The warm look of this room owes much to neutrals and the interesting textures of natural materials: the sunny pine of the floor (echoed by a compatible tawny shade of paint enveloping walls and ceiling) the basketweave chairs and the woven rug.

The affordable print of a Warhol original gives just the extra point of pink needed to keep the room scheme in balance; the blue ground also accentuates the anchoring effect provided by the sofa baseboard.

The sofa bed, a large long-term investment, has been used to cue the entire scheme. Its components are yellow, blue, pink, green and lavender against a pale ground. Everything else in the room takes its reference from this dominant piece.

Felicitous touches of bright yellow lead the eye from sofa cushion to cut chrysanthemums to the elegant cream drapes, giving an overall effect that is both chic and youthful.

The three armchairs match one another in shape, and tie in unanimously with the sofa. Loose covers give future flexibility.

The glossy white floor and white walls echo the white ground of the sofa print, accentuate the cheerful spaciousness and provide a good base for colour experimentation.

ACCENTS ON CHANGE

Familiarity is an important element in the comfort we derive from our homes. But beware of visual security becoming a bore; even the most conservative of homelovers needs the stimulus of change. Colour is the obvious tool to use to give an interior a quick and easy new look – to lift your spirits or match the seasons.

Using colour to provide novelty also affords an opportunity to experiment with it, to take chances, play games, invent new schemes and learn more.

Every room in the house offers opportunities for instant colour transformation: rugs, lampshades, loose covers, cushion covers and flowers in the living-room; table-linen and candles in the dining-room, and even dish-towels in the kitchen.

The accent green might more obviously have been introduced by using large, leafy indoor plants.

White is predominant in the room. The matt white of the walls is the starting point for an exercise in varying textures and quality: the soft white of the upholstery and drapes; the dull white of the canvasses; the many whites of the carpet; the paper white of the lampshade and the assorted whites of opalescent glass, candles and shells. Any of these elements could be almost any pastel colour, but subtle richness is achieved by this treatment.

Almost all the colours in the room are taken from this painting. The casual treatment it is afforded embodies the spirit of playing with colour. Hanging a sweater here totally changes the image and adds the colour of the garment to that of the décor.

The flowers, again, are deliberately cool pastel shades. More vivid blooms would give jewel-like brightness; more greenery or a large-leaved plant would cool the room and divide the two areas even more.

The cushions in the area take their coloration from the large wall painting. Any of its colours would work well together, depending on the effect desired: tones of blue for a more unified and cooler look; shades of yellow and gold for a prettier summer-time effect.

Most of the furniture is in varying shades of brown. Warm gold, green or deep red cushions would brighten the look of the sofas as well as softening their lines.

The set of inexpensive plastic tables, together with the waste-paper basket and box file by the desk, have been used to give a sharp accent green to the room. Deep beige plastic would have given a more unified look, while wooden tables would have provided a warmer overall feeling – particularly over an earthy multicolour rug.

The stone flags have set the basic earthy coloration of this interior. They impart a rural stolidity and coolness. In winter, a multi-coloured Indian rug, for instance, would both give immediate warmth to the room and change its coloration dramatically.

The floor cushions can give an instant change. A deeper and warmer look can be achieved merely by turning them over so that the burgundy ones are on top.

The small picture over the fireplace, which contains patches of strong blue, provides another colour source – allowing echoes of that blue in the interior, or suggesting strong contrast.

The lampshade in any other colour would accentuate the separation between the two seating areas. A strong blue, for instance, would make the fireplace area seem larger.

The cheerful greens and yellows of the cushions in this area here have been chosen as direct contrasts to the strong blue of the painting. These could be pastels, as in the rest of the room, for a more unified and serene look.

The white rugs maintain the cool elegance of the room. Burgundy rugs would add warmth, without jarring with the predominant pastels. Blue rugs, to match the fireplace painting, would unify the room by linking the two seating areas and would heighten the sense of sophistication.

The mirrored table and the glass objects on it add sparkle to the white of the room. The mirror would greatly amplify any colour placed on it – in candles or flowers – for a quick injection of colour.

MAKE BEDS, MAKE BEDROOMS

Bedspreads, quilts and linen lead particularly active lives as decorating accesories as, unlike more permanent furnishings, they have to be laundered and replaced regularly. Turn such chores into positive opportunities. Don't simply have several sets of sheets all in one favourite or harmonizing colour. Have a set in a contrasting colour for a dramatic effect, or in a bold primary colour for a startling mood change. Buy pillowcases in different colours from sheets to give yet more flexibility.

As bedclothes form such a large part of the colour story in the bedroom, it makes the perfect theatre for experimentation. The bedroom, being a private place, is the obvious site for a colour laboratory in which to test colour use and combinations before using discoveries more permanently in the public rooms.

Here in the same bedroom, with plain white walls and carpet, simply changing the sheets, bed-covers and accessories has created six quite distinctly different interiors. The changes shown can each be effected in a matter of minutes and the room could, if necessary, be changed again the following day.

In the same way you can create a special room for a newly-wed couple staying with you overnight; make a comfortable day-room for lounging and reading; or give yourself an exotic surprise on a weekend when you can luxuriate in change.

The linen chest has been covered by a red cord cloth – to give a strong texture and colour base – and covered with another patchwork crochet cover to amplify the 'colour clutter' effect. Any colour from the patchwork can be brought out and used in this way, or if the chest is a good wooden one, it can be left bare to bring out a country look.

The paintings and their frames lend a third 'patchwork' element. Such a set, in appropriate accent colours with coordinated frames, could easily be made from magazine covers.

A large patchwork bed-cover both sets the theme and allows any of its constituent colours to be used.

The white lampshades blend unobtrusively into the white on white and pastels.

The red cloth over the linen chest anchors the other colours in the room, but is muted by the diamond-draped lace cloth.

The white lace table-cloth like the pillowcases, is draped over a brighter pink cloth to give a similar suffuse effect. The other table-cloth is decorated with floral embroidery containing some small spots of strong colour to give sparkle.

The pillowcases have another set of pink pillowcases underneath them to produce a hazy pink seeping through to highlight the white-on-white print – this trick softens plain colours just as successfully.

The white floral brocade-effect sheets give a subtle base for a romantic setting: as would sheets in pastel colours. Most whitened colours harmonize: pale lemon and pink sheets, for instance, give an appealing 'sugared-almond' look.

The green and yellow table-cloths pick up the colours of the print in the same way as the bed-linen. If you do not have cloths in the right colours, use paper table-cloths in bold colours.

The table-cloths here have been thrown over a pair of matching linen chests, but tea chests, or even large packing boxes, can serve just as well when covered in this way.

A favourite, boldly coloured painting sets the coloration of this interior.

The deliberate contrast of the yellow, green and white used on the sheets, pillowcases, bed-cover and lampshades works equally well with the colours differently juxtaposed.

By using the same colours on different objects, the balance can be changed dramatically. Here, for instance, the bed is softened – almost camouflaged.

Indoor plants are perfectly suited to this coloration. Several large plants used with a green bed-cover would give a lush, jungle look; a large bunch of fresh daffodils might be the natural choice to herald spring.

The Polynesian block-printed bark cloth acts as an exotic theatrical backdrop to this sensual ethnic interior. Try making a block print on an old sheet, using poster paints.

The sheets, bed-cover and pillowcases can be any combination of warm browns, yellows or golds.

A large sculptural lamp from another room offsets the African carvings. If the white lamp bases had been kept, black or yellow lampshades would have worked well.

A woven blanket of the same period style as the Bauhaus stool also has a good earthy coloration, which successfully camouflages the stool.

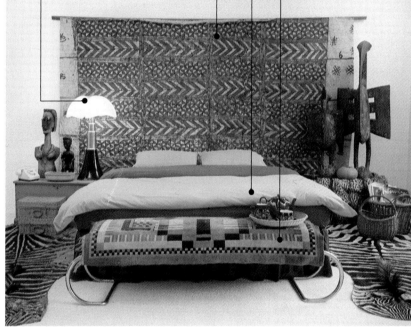

The bedside tables are terrace furniture, brought in at the end of the season and painted.

The plain black pencil drawings are massed to help give a low, horizontal look. Use a set of favourite black and white illustrations from newspapers or magazines.

A glossy black lampshade has been introduced and the other lamp replaced by a stylish desk lamp from the study to give sophistication.

The ashtray stands out as the only spot of accent colour.

The linen chests have been covered in lengths of cheap lining fabric.

A deliberate use of matt black on the pillowcases (or other black bed-linen) avoids any suggestion of sleaziness.

The chrome and black upholstered Bauhaus stool is the starting point for this interior.

It takes a good deal of courage to go for such a bold look, and the power of the black and white contrast needs careful handling so as to strike the balance between theatricality and comfort.

The magic element of such a look would be a surprise, brightly coloured undersheet – say a primary red – visible only when the cover is drawn back.

91

SHELF LIFE

The mantelpiece is the perfect place to give a room a quick transfusion of colour: any 'tablescape', prominent shelf or other focal point can perform the same function.

Such places make ideal theatres for colour experimentation. Try massing objects for their colour rather than displaying all your possessions at one time just because 'they are there'.

Instead, pack most of them away and bring out different selections with colour themes, as we have done, to endow the whole interior with a totally different character and invigorate it with a shot of fresh colour.

Notice, too, how much the nature of the colours used in our selection of mantelpiece displays affects the coloration of the whole room by subtly changing the quality of the light and lending a cast to the white of the walls.

The yellow and orange set, for instance, warms the background white, and the framed pink paper produces a general rosy glow which radiates throughout the room.

You do not necessarily need to have many props: coloured candles and sheets of paper or cheap prints can give effects as powerful as any of those shown.

The cheap, cheerful Indian painting's bold colour use gives a strong, warm look and demonstrates the balance that is the key to the secret of managing 'difficult' orange.

The mirror gives depth to the floral profusion, while adding sparkle. The maple and dull-gilt frame links it with the coloration.

The marquetry-inlaid wooden boxes provide elegant tonal variety and some sophisticated patterning. Stencil plain wooden boxes for a similar effect.

A bowlful of porcupine quills and a stylish vase, crowned with an ostrich egg, give touches of the exotic.

The textural variety of the browns and golds of dried flowers and grasses, set in a hand-painted vase and punctuated with pheasant feathers, forms the basis for this rich neutral arrangement.

The 1930s Clarice Cliff ceramics and the modern picnic plates at each end blend well together, and uncannily with the Victorian figures, to form a happy union really only linked by colour.

An earthy orange is the principal colour in the decoration of the Staffordshire figures – 'the tribal art of England'.

A striking black-framed Sonia Delaunay screen print provides a shock of strong colour. Any bold multi-coloured print will give the same effect.

The spontaneous calligraphic brush drawing provides a formal backdrop and gives shape and substance to the setting. A framed page of newsprint would be just as powerful.

The pared-down simplicity of this setting makes it ideal for experiments with colour accents – one red rose in either vase, for instance.

An assortment of cheap Victorian coloured glass and '30s ceramics gives a similar multi-colour look. It is not necessary to match particular colours from the print; it is the similarity of colour variety and level that makes it work. Create a totally different effect by picking out one colour and ranging a number of objects to match: this is a good way, for instance, to show off a collection of blue Bristol glass or even old green bottles.

The impact generated by the contrast of black and white is used here to make the most of two fine objects: a tall, white, etched glass Daum vase and a black, bubble Lalique vase emphasize each other's elegance. Any piece of fine white china paired with, say, a small black lacquer box would have some of the same drama.

The 'family portrait' helps to establish the formal look, and the subtly varying blues in the dress reinforce the colour of the plates.

The deep blue candles supply an essential framing element. The deliberate use of clear glass, instead of white ceramic, candlesticks lightens the effect and avoids an overly solid-looking mass.

The large Chinese plates set the coloration and the symmetry and classic simplicity of the arrangement.

The willow pattern soup tureen, brought in from the kitchen, lends a pleasantly casual note to the otherwise rigid formality.

A favourite collection of green Art Nouveau china is proudly ranged.

A sheet of paper, in a pink chosen to contrast with the green of the china, is framed like a picture. It has all the air of an expensive work of art, injects an instant shot of colour and sets off the china in an unusual and exciting way. The paper can be painted the appropriate colour or bought from artists' suppliers. An equally appealing effect can be achieved using a sheet of yellow or bottle green to harmonize with the colour of the china's decoration: let the room décor dictate the exact colour choice.

Alternatively, use various coloured papers to make a collage relating to the colours of objects you want to display, but which would otherwise lack a linking theme.

TOWEL POWER

We count on our bathroom to freshen us, but how often do we do the same for it? The bathroom is an ideal candidate for quick changes. It is not a place that you linger in for hours on end, so if you want to experiment with dramatic colours, this is a reasonable place to start. Even if you still prefer the traditional, all-white bathroom, you can have the fun of bright, exciting accessories – blinds, mats, soap-dishes – to be changed as often as you like.

Because most bathrooms are comparatively small in area, their appearance can be altered without a great deal of work or expense. You also have at your disposal one of the most flexible sources of colour a decorator could wish for – towels. They come in every shade imaginable, and with countless patterns too. Since they must be washed regularly and renewed periodically, you have continual, built-in opportunities for ringing the changes.

These building blocks of colour have the power to pull whole schemes together, or send them shooting off in different directions. Towels are the necessities which can easily become the mothers of invention.

The red-ochre gloss of door-trim and soap-dish makes them stand out as the warmest points, even though the colour has been used sparingly.

The porous tile wall balances the areas of white and grey beneath it and is a rewarding textural foil for the polished wood and porcelain.

The emphasis on neutrals and achromatics in the permanent features of this room makes it highly flexible when quick changes are desirable. Any bright colour could be introduced in the form of accessories and trim.

The classic white basin with rich, polished-wood surround is a high-quality starting point from which the room scheme could build in any direction. It has been placed in a colour context which makes it masculine without being overpoweringly so. It also attractively sets off the various natural and neutral accessories, such as wicker basketry, sea-sponge and coral.

The brilliant, canary yellow of the waste-basket has a dynamic impact on the entire room, playing off every colour in the scheme. It stands boldly against the moody, slate-grey panel beneath the basin, and picks out the gentler yellows in towel, folded face-cloth and toiletries, so that they form a nearly circular composition.

The toasty beige carpet makes for visual, as well as physical, warmth underfoot, and is versatile enough to accommodate different colour schemes in the future.

The stack of towels unites the colours in this scheme and makes even the grey look warm. Their effect is far more appealing than if all were the same.

94

Cheerful, deck-chair stripes on the window blind express the yellow theme in a neat pattern and unite the shower stall with the outer room area.

Black towels, with a larger stack of ivory on top, echo the basic, strong contrast between floor and walls. The small, extra note of black at this level helps to balance the room scheme and demonstrates how effectively towels can make quick but substantial changes in a bathroom.

The warm, apricot shade of the hair-dryer and adjacent towels is the richest colour in the scheme and relieves it of the harshness it might otherwise have projected. The small, round container on the top shelf and the soap duck are examples of useful, easy, unifying touches.

The unusual use of black, on the floor and radiator, gives this small area drama and strength without limiting the future choice of accessory colours.

A honey beige is the colour used most extensively and most permanently. The thoughtful choice of accessories has succeeded in making it look sophisticated rather than safe, and enabled it to stand alongside primary yellow without looking weak or muddy.

Red, white and blue combine to create a classic, sporting look that is perennially fresh. Keeping the French-blue, gloss woodwork, several different moods could be evoked simply by changing some of the towels. If the red and navy ones were replaced with pink, a pretty pastel scheme would emerge. Swap red for blue-grey and get a subtle, graduated range of blues. Change light blue for yellow to star the primaries. Or for a cool, marine effect, substitute a selection of light and dark greens and blue-greens for the red and white.

SPECIAL OCCASIONS

Celebrating special times – Christmas, Easter, birthdays, weddings, victories, reunions and farewells – provides an opportunity to give rooms the star treatment with colour. You are unlikely to redecorate entirely for the sake of one big bash, but you can make it look as though you have done so. On these occasions colour can be deliberately exaggerated – used in a way that sets the event apart from the everyday. Taking tones already present in the room as your cue, let accessories be the means to an eye-catching, heart-lifting scheme, suited to the time of day, the menu and the occasion itself. Light shades will flatter light meals; strong ones, more robust fare. Certain looks are inherently dramatic – monochromatic, for instance, with the theme repeated in a wide range of textures; or liberal sparkling metallic touches. Colour is the make-up kit when a room puts on its party face.

Red paint has made ordinary inexpensive folding chairs suddenly glamorous. They blend with the lush red décor, and their arrangement in small groupings around several red-draped tables enhances the intimate atmosphere created by the tented ceiling, while helping transform an ordinary dining room into a banqueting chamber. The crimson, tented ceiling is an exotic fixture – sensuous, mysterious and opulent, which may be played up or down. Here it dominates, the colour, dictating that of the furnishings below.

The fine-line design of the china is matched by the table-cloth and napkins. A special party atmosphere is conjured up by coordinating both coloration and motif throughout. The emphasis on light and lightness creates a uniquely elegant setting.

Rose-coloured glasses in luxurious profusion impart optimism and delight to a cool, chic scheme. Their delicate tint gracefully links the pastel walls and the pink pin-striped linen and china. Their gentle curves complement the tulips and the moulding on the doors of the cabinet behind.

The table settings revel in the maxim that you cannot have too much of a good colour – heaping red candles, pepper mills, flowers and dishes on solid red cloths.

Patterns coexist cheerfully with the Persian-style wallpaper, the floral border of the table-cloths and the bold, flowery plates all using red, but increasing the visual interest of the room.

The gleaming black background could be paint, lacquer, satin or oilcloth. Any solid colour would work as a base for such images, but in this particular context, nothing could equal black for impact.

The strawberry constellation encircles a lemon slice snipped to complement the starry theme. Even the napkins are folded in points, and the crystal, seen from above, forms a stellar pattern.

These cherubs are reproduction Victorian die-cuts or scraps. The flowers are cut from seed catalogues. Distributed across a heavenly blue background of paper or cloth, they make a variation on the theme more suitable, perhaps, for a young girl's birthday party. Paper plates and napkins in pink would complete the effect.

Super-heroes for supper: this idea for a children's party puts primary colours to work atop the happiest of hues – yellow. These are strips cut from comic books, but the technique could be applied to a wide range of subjects and special interests.

The scattered metallic stars, forming a magical milky way, create a highly theatrical effect, perhaps for a midnight soirée. They have the jubilant air of confetti – lavish and random – yet their genius is simplicity.

The star-sprinkled china is the starting point for this festive arrangement. Black and white mix-and-match plates give variety to this stunning, achromatic setting, where gilt embellishment is fun rather than formal.

Use colour for depth and dimension; transform a white paper cloth with a fern or leaf motif (use a real leaf as your stencil) and layers of spray paint. Flowers cut from folded squares of notepaper have been strewn over it to complete the 3-D look with a flourish.

MAKING A BREAK

When you are getting away from it all how much colour should you take with you? A great deal depends upon the location and the types of activities associated with your home away from home. Often the setting itself is the supreme attraction, and the decoration should pay it tribute. Because strong colour is stimulating, it could contribute to holiday high spirits; conversely, an utterly plain scheme might promote relaxation. Consider whether your idea of a break is essentially active or passive – or both. Your use of colour will be influenced by the facts that you are probably tackling an area smaller than your permanent home, using fewer expensive furnishings and placing an emphasis on low maintenance and on creating a casual atmosphere. There are opportunities to use colour more adventurously than at home. In a situation where you would hesitate to hang expensive artwork, why not paint a family mural, or try cheerful, Pennsylvania-Dutch-style stencilling? Let the surroundings proffer their own artefacts – be they shells, stones, pine cones or wild flowers – and let their delicate shades be your inspiration. In the same way, the neutral tones of building materials, of natural wood or stone, can exert a calming influence. For a refreshing recreational environment, you cannot go far wrong by letting Nature's palette be your guide.

The spare, unadorned expanses of pine and glass combine sophistication with informality, leaving a neutral canvas for Nature's incomparable artwork.

The understated composition on the coffee table creates a focal point, celebrating simplicity and texture – with no jarring hues to ruffle the tranquillity of the seaside setting.

The white and purple cushions, with their stylized motifs of waves and seagulls, use clean, bright tones to link the outside and inside living spaces.

Basketry abounds, in both practical and decorative contexts – the neutral shades of all the different styles harmonizing naturally and enhancing the homespun atmosphere.

The clear red of the table-cloth is matched in the overhead lamp and the banner behind the stovepipe, but the disposition of these elements still has an engaging, chance quality – fortuitous rather than forced – to suit a rustic retreat.

Green baize tops turn bushel baskets into side tables in this easy-going, potluck scheme.

Vast geometric planes of glass decorate this beach home with the blue and white of sky, sea and sand. The bold, angular construction and spatial play extol the bracing clarity of the environment.

The white walls, tile floor and ceiling play up the limitless wealth of natural light. From dawn to dusk, they subtly change colour with the sunlight, harmonizing with the panorama beyond the glass.

The worn Indian carpets hung on the wall lend the room a snug, lived-in feel. Their coloration gives warmth and links the neutral base with the primary accents of this interior.

The zinnias supply a glorious burst of hot, summer colour, happily holding their own in the formidable scale of this room. They have kept to the unspoken rule that Nature is the decorator here, but they seem aware that if anything can steal the show from such an immensity of blue, it will be a handful of their crimson petals.

The bamboo blind, covering open shelves to avoid an overly cluttered look, is a shade lighter than the plain wood walls and fits in perfectly with the neutral/natural base.

The white furnishings, both indoors and out, strike a sophisticated, luxurious note while discreetly avoiding any competition with the view. Mated with the large-scale, clean-lined architecture they suggest the urban chic of a penthouse and create the perfect showcase for the exquisitely bronzed.

ON THE MOVE

Colour is eminently portable. Boats, tents, recreational vehicles and the like, offer splendid opportunities to experiment with showy schemes you would not dream of living with full time; as well as the fascination of perfecting an environment in miniature.

Enjoy the theatrical sensation of designing a set, striking it, and designing another. Make use of comparatively cheap accessories – from towels and slip covers, to disposable picnic cloths and paper accessories. Items such as tents and sleeping bags – once available only in drab, often military, colours – are now manufactured in dazzling shades and even in prints.

When selecting colours you intend to take travelling, especially to be seen out of doors, bear in mind the influence of the elements – strong sun and rain, mud and sand. Pastels are accustomed to leading a sheltered life, secure from such ruinous effects. Bright primaries and sturdy neutrals are more practical on the move.

Interiors are a somewhat different story. The living quarters on boats and vehicles are necessarily confined; colour should make them as roomy as possible while never forgetting that they have to rough it.

As a general rule, there is much to be said for keeping mobile schemes simple; shooting off in too many directions will only dissipate the energy of your design.

After all, the idea is not to compete with Nature but to celebrate it. The decorative potential of such settings, so often given little or no conscious thought, will give great returns on a small investment of imaginative effort, making good times more memorable.

Learn to exploit its recreational capacity and you can have a field day with colour.

The dark-stained wood provides a strong neutral base for this scheme: a perfect foil for the colours of Nature, brought in by large stretches of window.

The glossy chocolate-brown accessories: overhead light fixture, corner spotlights and stereo headphones, as well as the window mouldings create smart highlights.

The chess set decides all the design moves in this studied mobile interior. It contains the key elements – neutral cream and chocolate brown, and the checked pattern – repeated in the upholstery and the rug.

A few blue notes: cushions, kettle, ashtray, maintain the overall cool of a scheme that successfully brings urban chic to the country.

Yellow and white seat covers, reminiscent ·of awnings and deck chairs, carry the same happy message – here is a place to sit in the sun. In the heat of summer, the cloth covers not only make a decorative seasonal change, but they save passengers from the ravages of hot seats.

The yellow cap is a reminder that this type of portable, transitory colour can echo your holiday wardrobe or complement your look for the season.

Wild flowers picked *en route* add an exquisite finishing touch to the alfresco spread.

Red napkins keep this mini-scheme coordinated. Let even the wine and picnic ingredients play a part in the overall design.

The red-and-white-checked tablecloth brings the jaunty *bonhomie* of a sidewalk café to this beach setting. It contrasts brightly with the sand, making it practical as well as cheerful, as, on a long beach, it makes home base easy to spot.

LIFTING THE SPIRITS

Rooms, like people, have personalities, which evoke particular responses from those who come in contact with them. Frequently, the principal demand made of an interior is that it should always produce a specific state of mind.

The busy executive may need a room that is guaranteed to provide total relaxation after a stressful day in the crisp corporate environment; the city-bound soul might crave a haven of greenery amid the urban grey, or all that one might ask of a room is that it never fails to lift the spirits of anyone who enters it.

There is much more to mood management than just clever low lighting: colour's powerful psychological effects make its strategic use a potent and flexible instrument.

On the bleakest morning in the depths of winter, breakfast in the sunny yellow kitchen will put spring in the step and, even on a rainy day, the multi-coloured room promises marmalade in the pot at the end of the rainbow.

The brightly coloured flowers produce a country-garden look, whereas the brown ceramic tiger says 'jungle' – coming in from the concrete one to an evocation of the real thing. This generates an entertaining tension, but the mood could easily be tipped either way by varying the use of such elements.

The lush profusion of indoor plants – hanging from the ceiling, covering the walls and framing the window – produces its own mood. Natural tonal and textural variations abound, and the many leaf shapes filter and dapple the light. For a similar effect without the expense, cut out leaf shapes from sheets of tissue paper in two or three shades of green and paste them in a scattered pattern across the window.

The yellow plastic chairs bring sunshine into the room and create a practical, family feel.

The wall decorations, mainly in yellows and contrast bright reds, have an appropriate cheerful, outdoor-activity theme.

The highly polished wood of the table echoes the sunny yellow and the clean functional look of the chairs. A less spare effect could be created by draping the table in a French-café-type red-and-white check tablecloth and tying yellow-striped cushions to the chairs. This would give the same warmth with a softer touch and a hint of the Mediterranean.

The white walls allow the foliage to stand out in contrast. Dark green walls would have a much more dramatic and mysterious look: the green of the plants merging into the green of the walls, giving the impression that the 'jungle' continued beyond.

The floral prints on both sofa and table-cloth have white leaf shapes on a green ground – an interesting counterchange with the natural foliage green against the white of the walls.

The bold blue of the walls has great impact in this tiny space. Blue is a receding colour and the gloss surface reflects more light, giving a dimension-enhancing effect. It is, however, the strength of this billiard-chalk hue which gives the room character.

The mirror is an obvious dimension-enlarging element which here throws more colour back into the room. Used in this position it reflects the upholstery and carpet tones in particular, to give the impression that the room continues around the corner.

The stripes in the upholstery evoke the fun of childhood, holidays and outdoor activity. The rainbow gradation gives a feeling of expansion in the small space.

The china and the paintings on the wall echo the rainbow motif. The extra coloration and, more importantly, the fact that the theme has been carried through with such verve, convey enthusiasm and a great sense of fun.

The joyous theme of the colours in the fabric appear in the covering on the floor. Using such a big pattern in a small room creates a subtle and clever optical illusion. It suggests that the room extends beyond the walls and that the 'real' room goes as far as the end of the pattern and farther. This reduces any sense of confinement.

SETTING THE TONE

A well-designed interior looks good, feels good, and efficiently performs its intended function.

The creation of the right mood is often an intrinsic part of such practical requirements and colour is the key mood-maker.

A 'day-person' or a family will probably make greater use of the lighter tones for many rooms; an habitual night owl or a young urban couple, generally not at home during the day, might opt for atmospheric deep coloration.

A nocturnal worker would probably prefer a bedroom that shuts out the bustle and brightness of the outside world so as to induce sleep at any hour; alternatively, what may be needed is a room that triggers alertness as soon as the blinds are lifted.

Those who entertain regularly could find a truly dramatic setting useful. Deploy the power and magic of the theatre to create vividly evocative backdrops by, say, creating an essentially monochromatic scheme.

Each colour has its own personality. Hot, cool, intimate, relaxed, busy – there is a palette to match your needs.

The white pottery, white painted furniture and tall doors, together with the gilt picture frames, add classical formality and a touch of grandeur.

Indoor greenery looks especially good against yellowed tones. Here it both softens the lines of the room and supplies a welcome element of freshness.

The pale ochre walls set the serene mood of the room.

The grey of the cushion covers is a striking example of neutral contrast.

The plaid of the glazed cotton bed cover has colour links with most of the other items in the room. It gathers together the sunshine colours which give the interior its warmth and stylish cheerfulness.

Matt-painted deep blue walls and ceiling create a restful, closed-in space that feels totally private and detached from the outside world.

The blue-tinted glass of the lamps softens artificial light and maintains the night-sky illusion.

The white floral print, used on the bedding, blinds, walls and curtains, pulls the room together to produce greater intimacy. It also softens what would otherwise be a rather severe monochromatic interior.

The shaded yellow of the woven blind and the drapes amplifies the natural lighting for a strongly sunny effect.

The wooden furniture provides a neutral accent. Its natural coloration provides warmth, and it works well with the woodland motif of the print.

Low lamps create intimate pools of light. The light falling on the rich red upholstery and purple carpet lends a 'magic carpet' effect – the black walls seem to recede like the night sky.

The black walls are in sharp contrast to the red, giving a rich, dramatic background.

The red-painted fretwork, used as shuttering in front of the windows and as partitioning, gives interesting and mysterious lighting effects and provides the keynote for the theatrical, oriental feeling. Frame and paint plain garden trellis to try out such an effect.

The black lacquer table, the glittering vases and shiny black lamps give an inner contrast to the vast expanses of red, adding sparkle and sophistication.

The Indian-style print used on the sofa and cushions heightens the sensuality of the interior. Fold inexpensive Indian bed covers over soft furnishings for a similar look.

The floral patterning works together with the large Indian painting – the flowers in the painting seem to grow out of the sofa print – to give an organic lushness.

POINTS OF INTEREST

In creating a room that is both comfortable and functional, one of the real arts of decorating is that of being able to lead the eye to a specific part of the room – or to lead it away from a difficult area – in order to enliven a comparatively dead spot, camouflage a fitting or a flaw, or ameliorate bad proportions.

Strategic use of a fine painting or sculpture or flower arrangement is an easy ploy, but care must be taken to present such things in the right position, with the right lighting—as an integral part of the overall composition.

Colour's power is invaluable in such an exercise. The degree to which a focal point contrasts with its surroundings will obviously determine how greatly it stands out.

A dramatic effect can be achieved with little experience; a bright red ashtray in a modern, achromatic setting will rivet the eye. On the other hand, a concentration of quieter tones may act as a visual well-head from which the rest of the room scheme gently flows.

Colour is the means by which focal points make the eye rest or revel.

The pure panache and free spirit of the perennial flower child characterize this arrangement. The heaping up of brilliant hues and textures creates a collage so vibrant that it looks as if, at any minute, it might even start to move.

Romantic oriental exotica – the glossy crimson lacquer fan, the irridescent peacock plumes – are a magnet to the eye, drawing attention to any problem area – corner, entrance hall, bathroom – in need of a lift.

Flowers and more flowers; whether hand-made, plastic, painted, potted or cut, they blend together. Vases are easily found at import shops and markets. They assist the massing of elements to give an intriguing, bazzar effect.

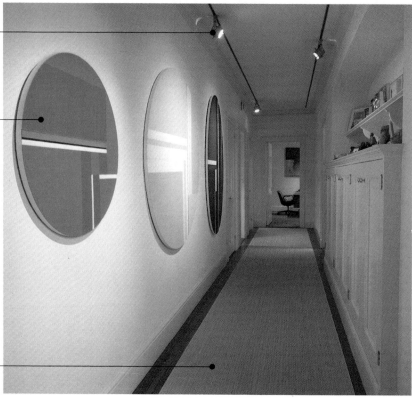

The spotlight tracks, which might have been camouflaged with the paint used on the ceiling, have, instead, been left conspicuous in a way that matches the dark floor edges—to comparable effect.

The carpet, rather than being fitted close to the walls, has deliberately been cut to leave space on either side, revealing the dark-stained wood floor. The two strong bands thus created act, in conjunction with the paintings, to keep the eye moving.

The trio of circular paintings in primary colours and the long, awkward hallway work wonders for each other. The paintings would be difficult to hang to best advantage in an ordinary room, but here they have the breathing space and sense of continuity they deserve. Their horizontal motifs and arrangement punctuate the space and lead the eye along to the room at the far end. Their primary coloration also gives them a serial, sequential identity, so that they reinforce one another as focal points. Their unusual shape and snappy brightness easily dispel monotony.

The flanking lamps, their marble bases, and the Roman blinds all serve a framing function, but in tones that are carefully muted so as not to distract too much attention from the painting itself.

The Japanese painting derives its hypnotic serenity as much from its formal coloration as its composition, with the branch curving in from the left, the raptor from the right, echoed in the rounded lines of the sofa frame, giving admirable balance to this handsome pier grouping.

The heap of subtly coloured cushions gives a gentle transition from the geometric floor to the figural print. It also spares the arrangement from appearing too rigidly symmetrical.

More a place to rest the eye than weary bones, this self-contained arrangement makes stunning use of what could easily have been dead space between two tall windows. It also proves that colours need not be florid to be fascinating.

The tiled floor, with its classic black, gold and off-white pattern, is arguably the starting point for this little scheme-within-a-scheme.

The deep green of the walls is enhanced by a lustrous gloss; both colour and texture are repeated in the satin sofa cushion, ruched blinds and candles.

The ceiling continues the elaborate trickery – a midnight-blue, star-spangled sky, only partially concealed by another casually draped, make-believe curtain. Precious space is gained by the illusion that, beyond the jewel-toned three-colour moulding, the room is open to the air.

The 'trompe-l'oeil' door treatment is the show-stopper in a room already brimming with richly saturated hues. The shimmering, gold-printed, vermilion silk image stands out stunningly from the wall – the slightly orange red is the perfect contrast to a somewhat blue green. Its effect is both to camouflage and accentuate the door at the same time.

The Indian painting, propped on the floor, calls to mind a culture where frankly fanciful colour combinations are part of the joy of life – another possible inspiration for the gleaming tones of the cornice, and for the theme of the room.

The boldly-patterned carpet is possibly the starting point of the room scheme, as there is more flexibility in the choice of paints to match furnishings than vice versa. The large pattern is a clever device for making a small space appear roomier – part of a greater unseen space.

ACCENTUATE THE POSITIVE

Colour can be used to celebrate shape: it might proudly outline structural elements normally disguised or treated in a conventional way; it might create a kind of benign tension, to unify large spaces visually without constricting them, or it might glamorize something utilitarian.

The difference between creating focal points and highlights is akin to the difference between cosmetic treatment which emphasizes the facial features such as eyes or mouth, as opposed to accentuating the bone structure. Whereas focal points stop the eye, highlights keep it moving. This is an area in which colour may cheerfully be flaunted for its own sake, used in an amusing, tongue-in-cheek fashion to give interest to a dull space or to establish a frame.

When planning highlights, remember that the greater the contrast to their surroundings, the more conspicuous they will be. Strongly expressed highlights are more suited to active rooms; for a peaceful atmosphere, keep the highlights discreet – they will still make a contribution, but one of reassurance rather than reverberation.

Take care not to let highlighting effects overpower your total design, or not upstage other features, unless that is your design. A good understanding of highlighting will always enable you to accentuate the positive.

The scarlet sink fittings make a feature of shapes we normally take so much for granted that they are rendered psychologically invisible. They show how easily colour highlighting can surprise us, simply by revealing what was there all along. The designer, having decided to use colour in what is commonly an achromatic context, chose the punchiest of all – a clear comment on the bold intention of the scheme.

The red band runs around this room for the sheer fun of it. It highlights the airiness and freedom of a generous open space. It also tangibly unifies the two sections of a large L-shaped room. Red itself is so bold, it perfectly suits such a provocative device.

The trio of coffee pots is more colour for pure amusement. In a room making a point of mixing kitchenware, toys and art, the pots are not alone in taking on the characteristics of all three.

The huge checkerboard motif on the sliding door adds to the playful atmosphere, taking its cue from the trivet on the table, which in turn is partnered by the pattern blocks. The emphasis on geometric shapes and primary colours gives the room energy and graphic impact.

The red grouting not only reinforces the sink fittings for a slick, custom-made-ensemble appearance; it gets design mileage out of lines that are usually scarcely perceived. The result is a striking, checked, graph-paper look. If the tint you want is not available, you can always add pigment to ordinary white grout.

Raise high the roofbeams by painting them green, and your spirits will rise as well. This imaginative treatment of the structural elements (including pillars and rafters) emphasizes the happy feeling of wide open spaces. Green is the brightest colour in this overall scheme, inspired by the freshness of its woodland setting. While green is not a natural shade for beams, it does evoke foliage and looks pleasing juxtaposed with broad expanses of plain wood. Its use in this way is bold, picking out the important lines with broad strokes that have the youthful bravado of a crayon drawing. A consistency of line has been achieved by making the sides of the open staircase in a width precisely matching the upstairs floor-support beams. Clever highlighting has made this a delightful tree-house for grown-ups.

The blue railings are a secondary highlight – fine lines in comparison to the hefty green. Both their colour and their metal-pipe construction add a high-tech note to this modern-day cabin. The blue is reiterated in accents such as cushions, window frames, upstairs shelving and downstairs door. Like green, blue figures prominently in Nature's palette, but here both have been used in an abstract – rather than literal – way.

The dark brown upholstery and carpeting is an obvious earth tone; both a good foil for the brighter highlights, and an appropriately practical choice for a country retreat.

SETTING LIMITS

Colour has the capacity to guide, inform, set limits and define function. In public facilities and in industry, the concept of colour coding is widely used to give instant direction and to call immediate attention to danger zones.

A more aesthetic application of the same basic set of principles can produce equally effective results in the home.

There are times when you want to give a specific working identity to a limited space: colour can be an effective partition – the shape it creates can have intrinsic visual interest as well as serve a practical purpose.

By decorating with ingenuity you can subdivide without the need for physical barriers, or give distinction to an adjacent area without cutting it adrift from the general scheme. Let your choice of stand-apart colour relate to the interior as a whole.

Colour's ability to establish order, to invent space-within-space, is one of its most satisfying attributes; learn to control it and you will find that you can virtually enlarge your home from the inside out.

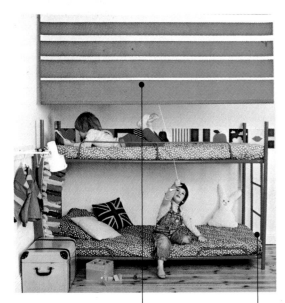

The green and white blind defines a sleep and play area for children – in the colour of youth itself.

The red frame of the bunk frames a space as well. It also gives a context for the use of cheerful primaries.

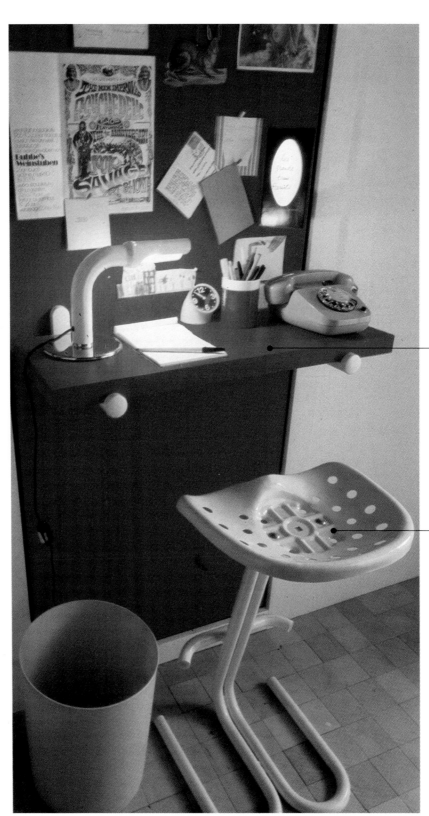

Red creates a mini-office in the area between two doors. The bold band of scarlet sets this active zone apart as effectively as curtains, doors or screens – without losing a scrap of either precious space or light. Painting the wall and desk/shelf in one smooth stripe of red has established both identity and order. A forceful single shade – red in particular – seizes attention, radiates energy and all but declares aloud 'Go to work!' It also helps visually to keep tidy a space that will inevitably succumb to periodic chaos. The inspired efficiency of this set-up, which could so easily have been no more than an ordinary, awkward wall-phone and pinboard, owes everything to the practical application of colour.

The white accessories – lamp, brackets, waste-basket and tractor-seat stool – blend in well when seen against the white walls, thus reducing any potential clutter. They also share a modern, curvilinear design, adding to the neat, appealing, but no-nonsense, appearance of this space-effective arrangement.

The dining-room walls are painted a luscious wine red to create an identity altogether separate from that of the living-room. Red is intimate, stimulating and heated. It is used extensively in restaurants because of its ability to spark appetites and conversation.

The painting's hues give it a provocative intensity quite distinct from its counterpart in the living-room, even though both are related by their contemporary style and their subject matter.

The vibrant, multicoloured flowers charge their surroundings with a dynamic, whereas the monochromatic freesias, on the table in the foreground, evoke airy calm.

The modern/primitive cushion covers enliven the living room, and their strong mulberry stripe sets up a link with the dining-room.

The ivory sofa and chair, with their solid tone, increase the sense of space and provide the right, simple setting for the boldly patterned cushions.

The serene, olive-neutral walls of the living-room, taking their cue from the gentlest shade in the carpet pattern, have a relaxing, expansive effect,

The overall scheme of the living-room is light and spacious – its openness enhanced by an entire wall of mirror. Colour defines this calm space as passive rather than active – in contrast to the adjoining dining-room. The ethnic qualities of the furnishings link both rooms, but the deeper, stronger tones in the alcove mark it for briefer periods of use.

GETTING IT TOGETHER

Why is it that certain interiors work so well, their whole appearing greater than the sum of their parts? The trick is continuity and the medium is colour.

This does not imply that unity may be achieved only by painting everything one camouflaging shade. The most subtle and satisfying effects are the result of various key colours recurring in imaginative permutations of texture and context.

Attention to detail is what gives coherence to an area, even if, as in the case of one-room living, many functions are required of the same, limited space.

In open-plan – or even just open-door – interiors, it is often desirable to provide a visual link from one area to the next. By employing colour in overlapping themes or motifs, you can establish this progression and still enjoy areas with individual characters. The accent colour in one place may be the main colour in another, leaving scope for new colours to be introduced.

The skilful devising of connections through colour is invaluable in pulling an interior together. This is where your design investment pays interest at a compound rate.

The buttery beige, featured on the double central panel and outside trim of the shutters, as well as on the window frame and main door, has a special unifying function. It is the only one of the pastel shades to bear a family relationship to those other important elements of the room's coloration – the warm, sunny, brown cork floor; the ochre-yellow throw rug, and the cocoa chair and sofa suite. Although the room has an overall soft pink feel, this golden connection also serves to hold it together. This is quite essential when the shutters are open – showing only beige frames and edges.

Pastels and panache combine to create a delicate, but clearly defined, small-scale interior. The effect is warm without being crowded; feminine without being frilly.

The chest of drawers and the folding chairs discreetly reiterate the pastel-stripe motif. Its thematic use contrives to break up space in an interesting but unaggressive manner, while at the same time providing continuity.

The large expanse of louvred partitioning which hides away the clutter of one-room living – kitchen, bathroom and storage – is itself camouflaged by being painted in gently varying pastel shades to give a mural-like effect.

The satin pillows illustrate the way that texture and finish, rather than brighter or contrasting colours, can be used as accents in such a scheme. The same pinks, mauves and greens, seen in matt paint throughout the room, used on the pillows in this way catch the eye with their light-reflecting sheen.

The secret inspiration for the entire room scheme may well have come from the pastel-striped bed-linen, which virtually fills the small room once the sofa bed is open. It even contains a cocoa-coloured band to link it to the upholstery.

Even the television must not interrupt the quiet flow of pastels; hence its casing in a plastic 'shade of pale'.

The lavender kite adds a welcome cool note, balancing the pink and yellow window alcove. In this context it forms a casual composition, linking that area with the multiple pastel theme of the room.

The walls are painted in an interlinking scheme which, without seeming contrived, gives the area coherence. The large, light-yellow wall shows the painting to best advantage and maximizes the already generous play of sunlight. The blue wall of the passageway lifts its tone directly from the painting and is accented by the small yellow window surround – which, in turn, could be seen as framing the outside view like a little canvas. Blue and yellow have been orchestrated throughout so that both kitchen and passage introduce one another equally well. They both, however, stand complete on their own, even without the visual link.

The large painting contains all the clues to the treatment of this dining-room and its adjoining passage. Its free use of blue, and blue patterns, is reflected in the china and patchwork cushions. Its snippets of clear yellow cause the eye to constellate them with the boots and coffee pot in the hallway. Its abstract style creates a balance between traditional and modern reflected in the decoration as a whole. The terracotta plant pots share old-fashioned colour and texture values with the time-worn stone flags in the passage.

THE PRIMAL THEME

A strong colour theme can do more than unify interiors; it can tie a whole home together. This does not necessarily mean treating each room identically; but, instead, relating them in a way which gives the whole scheme real vitality.

Keeping to a particular range of colours, shift the emphasis to match the individual character of each area, and take advantage of different contexts and varying textures.

Colour used in this purposeful way rewards with an aggregate power and resonance.

The way in which linking themes are applied varies with the nature of the premises. If space is confined, good visual links can keep the eye travelling, making the proportions appear more generous. If the spaces involved are uncomfortably large, the repetition of strong motifs will knit them together. Undistinguished architecture or location can be redeemed by this type of imaginative personal stamp. Such confident treatment is an excellent way to use colour to prepare a home for presentation for sale.

In your existing decoration there are probably themes with the potential to be developed and used more widely. Look closely; perhaps all that is missing is a link.

Tame wide open spaces with a bold theme. Strong colours do appear to advance, but in large rooms you can use a primary-laden paintbrush over large expanses without fear of causing claustrophobia. The eye then naturally draws the interior together, and rich shades will warm up surroundings not inherently cosy or snug. If you prefer a less aggressive approach, but still want the fun of brilliant hues, make your links through highlights such as baseboards, windows and door-frames.

Whether the quantities used are great or small, repetition of intense colour makes the connections that conquer space.

Space itself has a hygenic effect; so there is no need in this lofty bathroom for the traditional sanitizers, blue and green. What is required is a warm embrace – and that is a job for red.

The white towels and shower curtain would be ideal foils for this expanse of red, even if a different shade was partner to the red in the rest of the house. Nothing can match white for sheer clean freshness, and the bold contrast with red shows off the white to perfection.

The grey industrial flooring is immensely practical and comfortable, both physically and visually. It does nothing to detain the eye on its upward journey, sets off the red without fighting it and, as an achromatic, is analogous to the black used structurally elsewhere.

The matching gloss-red accessories: lavatory seat and cleaning brush; towel rail; shelves and baby's changing table, keep the scheme simple, strong and pure. All are naturally paired with, or seen in contrast to, white. This keeps the room in balance, and unites it with the house as a whole.

The white walls exalt the splendid attributes of light and space in this tall converted barn.

The black support girders are featured in a way that highlights the structure of the building and, in concert with the red and white, evokes a painting in the style of Mondrian.

The red cabinets and partitions define those features which have been added to the original white structure. The colour has been controlled so that these broad canvasses share a common height, breaking up the dramatic distance from floor to ceiling with an effect comparable to wainscoting. The impression given by the solidly built partitions is almost theatrical – as if they were stage flats and could be moved around with ease. They preserve the air of freedom while defining areas for different uses.

The rich gilt of the frames, and the paintings themselves, humanize the almost awesome environment, and are displayed to advantage against red – a technique employed by many major museums and galleries.

The polished wood floor flows freely throughout, unifying the various spaces. In a diplomatically neutral way, it also provides an uncompetitive base for the aggressive colour scheme and for the use of dark- and light-stained wooden furniture.

Rugs, like islands, mark out functional areas, their red backgrounds echoing the walls.

COOL CAMOUFLAGE

What can you do if you wish your house to have a free-wheeling, open-plan design, yet cannot give up the privacy and convenience of separate rooms? Use colour to get the best of both worlds: try decorating walls in similar light tones throughout. Techniques such as stippling, dragging or using fine graduated stripes – all of them more densely shaded at the bottom and lightening toward the ceiling – will give height to a room and, if necessary, can also serve to mask badly plastered or otherwise flawed walls.

To increase the airy, spacious feel, you can camouflage furniture in the same way: by making it recede and blend into the background you reduce visual clutter in a confined area.

Often a single floor covering is used throughout a home purely for reasons of economy, but this can also be a real decorative boon as it lets the eye travel unimpeded from space to space. Even in individual rooms, wall-to-wall covering of the floor is the most space-enhancing treatment, the more so if it is kept plain and pale.

Stronger coloured rugs can always be used to mark out functionally separate areas.

This cool, airy living room embodies all the important design themes used throughout the house to foster sensations of peace and space.

The delicate grey-blue-on-white drag-painting, applied comprehensively to ceiling, walls and furniture, has the dreamy, sun-bleached feel of driftwood: its tone a gentle echo of the surrounding sea and sky. The rush matting in a neutral, sandy shade flows uninterrupted into every corner of the house, making the whole appear roomier.

Other recurring motifs include the arc and circle shapes, reminiscent of boat hulls and sails; shells, both natural and artificial, and recessed, or subdued, lighting.

The sofa upholstery subtly reaffirms the drag-paint colours, with its one or two cushions shaded in the ghostly blue of the inside of a mussel-shell as a refined accent.

Vertical striping applied to the cabinetwork creates a theme-within-a-theme by making more dynamic use of the drag-paint colours. It provides visual interest while expanding the dimensions of the room.

The cobalt-blue vase, perhaps unremarkable in a more vivid setting, is positively riveting in this context. It is a deep, true blue, straying to neither green nor purple – rather an intensified form of the drag colour and, as such, a simple but glorious accent.

Neutral accents, in the form of glass and shells, link the room to the general scheme. A fetching touch is the slim blue candle in a bottle which matches the vase.

Even the folding chair has been given the enveloping drag treatment – its slats a felicitous echo of the stripes.

Bedding, diagonally striped in the drag-paint colours, has a fresh, nautical feel. These lines also have the effect of making the beds look bigger.

Even the tiles on the wall have been painted to remove the unnecessary diversion they might otherwise create. The overall colour of the scheme has the same cool clean effect of tiling and is a particular boon in this, the hottest room in the house.

The work alcove is lit by fluorescent light so that it stands out, although it is decorated entirely within the established, house-wide pattern. This makes it a focal point within the room and picks it out as an area of activity.

The fridge/freezer, as well as the front panels of both sink and dishwasher, clearly demonstrates the superb camouflaging effects of both the dragging technique and of a universal theme, It causes these bulky items to recede rather than obtrude, giving a welcome air of freedom in the room that needs it most.

The blue-rimmed glasses sound a discreet accent note, linking them to the vase and candle in the bunk bedroom.

The gas stove and adjoining sink are the most pronounced area of stainless steel, but this gleaming achromatic is so well suited to the whitey-blue that it is celebrated in such functional accents as the ventilation tube and the regiment of coffee pots. Even door handles and utensils have a design role.

The white blinds with blue-grey trim express the key notes of the scheme through coloration: blurred but firm lines and hazy, filtered light.

The mirror is framed in drag-blue to reflect exactly the circular motif on the bedspread. Its placement is decidedly decorative and space enhancing, rather than practical. The recessed lighting is passive and warm, in keeping with fixtures elsewhere in the house.

The shells on display are almost a treasure trove to which other shells, scattered throughout the house, have been leading. All are white, whether pearl-like or chalky in texture, so that sheer form becomes their salient quality. The collection accentuates the dream-like, underwater spirit of this relaxing scheme.

The blue drag-painting of the ceiling and walls is so perfect a match to the treatment of the living-room that it is scarcely noticeable that the former is plaster, while the latter is tongue-and-groove wood. This is where a linking theme comes into its own – exercising its ability to mate rooms of varying function and even of different building materials.

The bed-linen adheres neatly to the drag-paint colours, the diagonally striped pillow-cases matching those in the bunk-bed room; the circle motif recalling that in the living-room as well as the mirror above.

FAMILY TIES

A linking theme may be as subtle as a series of prints, consistent in style or subject, similarly framed and mounted, a few of which are displayed in each room.

A theme can even be developed by simply using natural colours and textures to give a country feeling to a town house.

Varying the proportions in which chosen linking colours are used from room to room, and changing the particular uses to which they are put, can produce fascinating effects. If you have used great expanses of a key shade in one area, you might confine it to baseboards or door- and window-frames in another.

This type of linking theme can act as a diversionary tactic, directing the attention away from problem areas. The interior becomes a focus of interest in its own right.

A sense of adventure arises from the way the theme is varied from room to room. It is not unusual for there to be more than one theme at work, but let any minor themes support, rather than upstage, the main one.

Once you have control of this type of approach, you can achieve unity without any risk of sacrificing versatility.

Beams painted white, to blend in with the ceiling and walls, become part of the pure and simple backdrop for this scheme, where primaries have the starring roles in each scene.

The blinds form blocks of colour, unmatched with one another, yet creating the vital link with the other rooms by stating the theme of primaries.

Brick-red gloss picks out the metal struts on this internal partition separating the kitchen from the dining area. It is used consistently on all window framing, thus establishing a minor linking scheme.

Neutral accessories, such as the cane seats and bamboo place mats, give a natural touch and keep the atmosphere fresh and modern, without interfering with the primary theme.

The gleaming doors use primaries in bold blocks; the entire aspect of the hallway changes as each door is opened or closed.

The bed-linen, with fine undulating lines in primaries against a white ground, maintains the colour story with both discretion and vitality. The bed is such a prominent feature in this small space, the colour statement has to be kept quite muted. The changing of proportions of primary usage is the key to keeping the theme lively – achieving harmony without monotony.

The amusing collection of *objets trouvés* on the shelf behind the bed is less random than it might at first appear; a second glance reveals that all the items have neutral coloration so as to fit in with the secondary theme of accents and accessories.

The large plants incorporate green into the scheme; they contribute to the conservatory atmosphere in an apartment that makes generous use of foliage and glass. Although green has occurred as part of the main linking theme in the other rooms, here it is expressed only in its natural state.

The strong colour used throughout on metal framing here calls attention to the fine vertical lines of this floor-to-ceiling window. This causes the eye to travel upwards, and helps give the maximum sense of space in a comparatively confined Paris loft.

The wall hanging of fabric art takes up the supporting neutral theme in a positive way. It naturally echoes the block motif seen elsewhere in blinds and doors, but in no way conflicts with the room's main attraction. The result is a simple reversal of the usual order, whereby the furniture has become art and the art has become a functional means of breaking up space, as well as providing a quiet resting place for the eye.

The vibrant print covering the sofa and armchair is the most resounding expression of the primary theme – truly *fortissimo* compared with, say, the bedroom's *piano*. As the extreme end of this scheme's dynamic range, it plays at exciting full volume; yet it remains perfectly in balance.

The light pine floor links the living-room to the dining-room, opening up space with its smooth, clear expanse.

Colour crafts

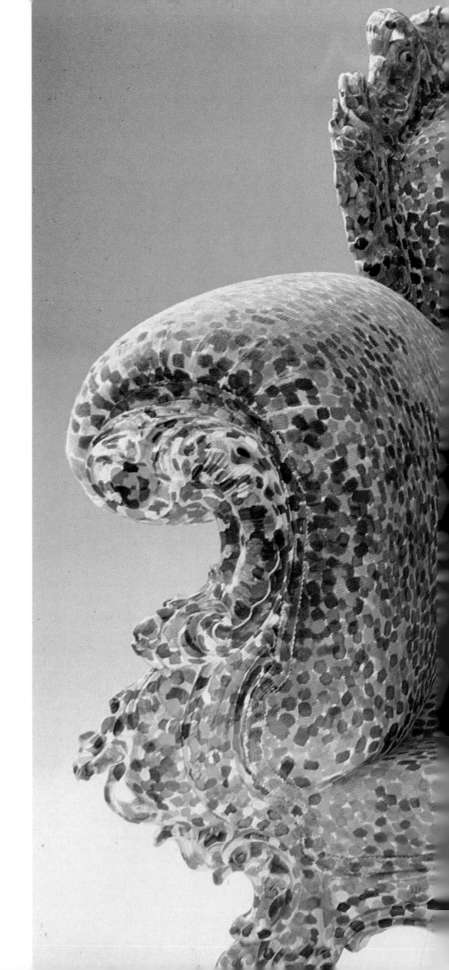

It takes some initial courage to break away from plain paints or commercial wallpapers, but once you tackle the more adventurous end of decorating – crafts or 'special effects' – you get more than you pay for: in style, originality and fun. Some of the techniques are quite literally child's play, but the savings and satisfaction are serious considerations. Deciding – daring – is the first step, and often the hardest. Even professionals admit to bouts of stage fright, but a successful stipple or stencil can become habit-forming.

Experiment on an area where you have nothing to lose; flawed surfaces can be camouflaged and at the same time given new interest with, for instance, a colourful combed pattern or clever collage. You might start with just a door frame and be inspired to continue around the room, as suddenly simple walls become the canvas for your art.

Stippling and sponging are basic abstract finishes which are both attractive in their own right and versatile elements of more complex techniques, such as antiquing or the subtler, modelled type of stencilling. Spattering and dribbling are akin to 'action painting' and give a room real vitality. Combing and dragging have a long history – methods so spontaneous they have been practised by primitive Africans and enthusiastic Victorians alike. To achieve wood-grain and marbling effects that are truly *trompe-l'oeil*, you would need to become apprenticed to a master craftsman – or hire one: but the amateur can produce imaginative and pleasing variations in colours Nature would envy. If you prefer a technique with guaranteed control and finesse, try stencilling – for results that run the gamut from cheeky to chic. Collage is a skill worth reviving from student bulletin-board days; it remains a treasure trove of personal expression.

In applying any of the following colour crafts you are assured individual, made-to-order, one-of-a-kind results.

The flamboyant form of this ornate armchair has been matched with a glorious overall multicolour stipple paint-job, replacing gilt and plush with joy and surprise.

STIPPLING AND SPONGING

Get smart with paint. Once you step beyond the simple, solid finish you enter a world of painted textures – flecked, mottled, crackly, nubbly, grainy – alive with the play of light and shade. They have the advantage over wallpaper in that they are always original and free of any rigid pattern repeat. You can apply them in any colour combination you like and can even control what might be called their dynamic range – making the pattern denser or more deeply coloured to draw attention to certain areas, perhaps, or diluting it near the ceiling to give the room a lift. The purposely fragmented quality of these finishes also makes them ideal for disguising flawed surfaces, both in rooms and on furniture.

Of the many techniques possible using broken colour, the easiest to master and the speediest to effect are stippling and sponging – dabbing on paint with the tips of brushes and sponges respectively. Special, stiff-bristled stippling brushes are sold by painters' and decorators' suppliers; however, cheaper brushes, as well as textured rollers or even wads of different cloths can be equally effective. A genuine sea sponge gives a more interestingly varied effect, but a coarsely porous artificial one can give more dramatic results. For a crackly finish, a handful of bunched-up plastic bag will serve.

For further effect, mask surfaces to leave stripes or other silhouetted motifs of the ground colour. The results may be left matt, but a coat of clear varnish will both protect and lift the colours.

An all-over treatment with a uniform stipple pattern here gives a fresh, boundless feel – the varying hues blending to produce an aquamarine effect. Pipes, odd angles and mouldings are all evenly blanketed in the flurry of blue. This particular finish was achieved by use of a machine. Contractors with heavy-duty spray guns can be hired to give high-speed application of the colours of your choice. It is necessary simply to mask off or remove anything not due for the treatment. Using a mixing device, the spray can be supplied by more than one can of paint, so that several colours may be applied simultaneously in varying proportions.

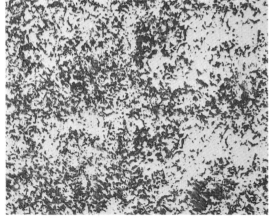

A crisp contrast of two greens, the dark stippled over the citrusy light, gains extra vitality from the blur of movement where the brush has slipped slightly.

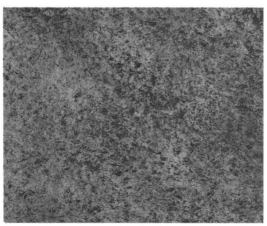

Mood indigo. Finished with a fine spatter, this downy, tone-on-tone stipple derives its depth from a dry-brush application of inky blue over a mottled azure ground.

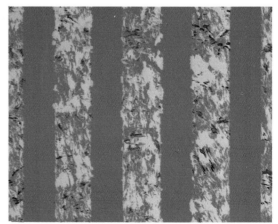

Ochre and flecks of black neutralized with blue have been dabbed with a dry brush on a red ground, which has been covered with regularly spaced strips of masking tape. Curiously, when the tape is removed the effect seems the reverse – that the red strips have been applied over an already stippled base.

To achieve a crackle texture, use a crinkled-up plastic bag to daub paint over a base colour. This gives a quirky, random pattern which can be used to cover large wall areas quickly. Here it is applied thickly, in a warm scheme of yellow and pink over an ochre base. Its deliberate unevenness relates it to the wood grain.

The mantelpiece, with its lighter base colour, has had paint slapped on in a bold fashion that echoes the large-scale, crackle pattern on the wall.

The crackle treatment is speedy, dramatic and a good camouflage for flawed walls and woodwork. A medium base shade lets either darker or lighter overtones give depth.

An optical illusion – not pink sponged on a pale ground – but actually a flat-brushed, deep pink base with a pale, tonal pink stippled finely over it, and cream sponged on top.

A close-textured, luminous dove-grey sponge finish on a pale grey base is given an almost subliminal lift with a scattering of tiny, primary-coloured dots.

123

SPATTERING AND DRIBBLING

Nothing matches the sheer vitality of 'action-painted' surfaces. They look so lively because they record sharp, speedy – sometimes violent – gestures, propelling paint at a surface; quite unlike the smooth, passive motion of a brush or roller taking paint directly to it. The principal craft techniques involved are generally known by the unappealing but descriptive designations of 'spattering' and 'dribbling'.

The look instantly evokes the work of the American painter Jackson Pollock, internationally recognized for his huge, abstract paintings of the late 1940s and '50s, created by trickling colour over canvas. The resulting lines twist and intertwine in spontaneous, free-flowing shapes and patterns. The delicate, filigree webs and thick, rich swirls of colour marked a new attitude toward paint as well as a new style of painting. The compositions have a strong, meditative character, with no discernible beginning or end. The fresh style readily influenced fifties designers of textiles, wallpapers, linoleums and carpets.

To experiment with spattering and dribbling, first try the techniques out on a sheet of wall-lining paper.

If the treatment is eventually to be used on the wall, tape the paper to a wall – gravity makes the effect of the action altogether different on a vertical as opposed to a horizontal surface, such as a floor or table.

During both experiments and eventual decorating, make sure that areas not meant to be painted are well masked. To spatter, load a dry brush with thick paint, and with a quick flick of the wrist you are in business. The flow of paint is even easier to control when dribbling patterns on a floor or other horizontal surface.

For distinct colours, let each one dry before applying the next. For chance blends, proceed while paints are still wet.

These bathroom walls show how the diagonal drift of an action spatter on white walls is suggestive of marble. To produce this effect, the paint was flicked on with a long, and quite natural, diagonal arm movement. First with the black; then, in smaller quantities, the grey; and finally little accents of turquoise to send a zing through this otherwise stark achromatic scheme. A narrow, black-painted border tidies up the edges and gives the room a more tailored look.

The textured, solid black industrial rubber flooring is an ideal foil for the treatment of the walls.

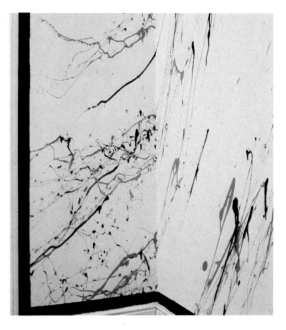

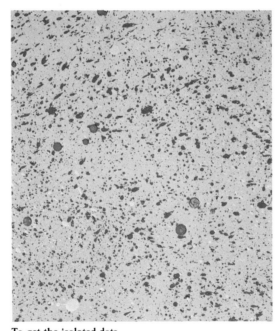

To get the isolated dots seen in this multicolour spatter, it is advisable to use paint of comparatively thick consistency, thus avoiding drips. Darker and lighter contrasting flecks over a bright, medium-toned ground seem, to the eye, almost to vibrate, suiting this look to accents such as old radiators, frames or small furniture.

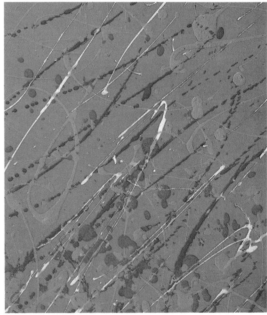

The 'Jackson Pollock look', with exuberant, skating dribbles, has been achieved by swinging a thickly-loaded paintbrush over the surface in rapid loops and zig-zags. Contrasting blues with green gain extra definition from a highlight of white. For added impact, the dribble colours have also been spattered over the result.

DECORATIVE FINISHES

Spontaneity is what makes the many decorative paint finishes special; each is emphatically the product of the creator, as personal as a signature.

Consider the possibilities of finishing with a flourish. Glaze or wash surfaces with a thinned-down version of the base or another colour entirely. Such a finish gives depth, and can cool or warm the base. Here a casual, slapdash style with the brush can give positive results.

Layering colours or varying shades also gives the opportunity to create a whole new range of paint colour effects by taking away the colour you first thought of. Just drag a dry brush through a thin wash to give an interestingly aged look, or create original patterning by pulling a decorator's comb

through a high-contrast top coat. The materials needed for these techniques are assorted combs, brushes, rollers and rags – nothing too complicated. Courage to experiment is your most invaluable tool.

If you have no previous experience with any of these techniques, or if you wish simply to test how they will look in a particular room, have some trial runs. If it is the walls that are to be treated, it is essential to carry out trial painting on a vertical surface, using large sheets of paper pinned to the wall, rather than working on the flat, for brush strokes and the play of light appear quite different. By combining techniques and working in multiples of colour, there is no limit to the custom-made effects you can achieve.

The delicate, tawny rose tint washed over these white walls warms the environment so effectively that this city loft feels more like a Turkish hideaway – the romanticism heightened by the softness of the texture. Colour-washing lets the pale background shine through a greatly thinned, water-colour-like top glaze, which has been applied with a broad brush or sponge.

Unusual walls and ceiling invite an unusual treatment. The moody atmosphere of this vaulted structure has been enhanced with a type of antique glaze. A dark oil varnish or glaze, rich in pigment but loose in consistency, has been thrown – virtually rained – on the old-gold, ochre base and left to run. The glowing, almost tortoise-shell result ideally matches the blind.

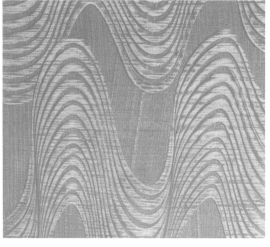

This dramatic comb pattern has an almost musical rhythm. Combing is an historic craft technique, practised in many contexts – from African tribes incising designs into wet clay walls with bundles of sticks, to Colonial Americans painting special effects on furniture, baseboards or doors. The usual method is to prepare the surface with a light base coat, followed, when that has dried, by a deeper-toned, slow-drying, second colour. Pulling a comb through it makes patterns in the top colour since the base coat shows through. A professional decorator's comb is normally flat-toothed rubber, but a home-made one of stiff cardboard or plastic can be notched to any desired width.

Drag painting is one of the staple, simple textured finishes. This tone-on-tone turquoise is an example of how brushes may be used to remove colour as well as apply it. The paler shade is the base (which is usually a flat colour but here has also been dragged) over which the deeper shade has been applied and then partially removed, using a dry brush. This gives the appearance of a natural fibre or grain.

This specialized multicolour drag has been achieved with small brush strokes, in a straight up-and-down movement. It is a relatively easy, if time-consuming, technique which permits walls or furniture a customized colour match to patterned fabric. This sample is composed of three different blues and three pinks or ambers. Where blues and ambers have overlapped slightly, there are little touches of green. Alternatively, you can apply the colours with a wet rag, which blurs and blends them gently as you go.

Antiquing: colour can be employed in a number of ways to persuade the eye that new wood is antique, or at least has the mellow, subtly variegated appearance of age. Antiquing may be simulated by applying different layers of colour, then partially removing them. A random spatter of a dark neutral shade resembles the freckles characteristic of old painted surfaces. Transparent glazes tinted with dulling greys, umbers or even dilute black, lend a finishing patina of imaginary years. This sample of Italianate antiquing was primed and undercoated, and given a coat of orange shellac. Four colours were then slapped on – two pinks and two greens. These were distressed with patches of paint stripper, wiped off once it had eaten through to the shellac. A glaze was applied and allowed to dry, then the whole thing rubbed with wire wool.

The more colours used throughout the process, the prettier the end result.

127

FINISHING WITH THE GRAIN

Although Nature holds the copyright to the lively patterns in wood, they may be freely adapted to embellish any surface that will take a glaze – and in colours Nature might envy. Exact, *trompe-l'œil* wood graining is a matter for experts, but the amateur can improvize any number of fetching, fanciful finishes.

Begin by looking closely at real wood. Each piece graphically records incidents from the parent tree's life story. Here the grain streams vigorously around dark knots, signifying the birth of a branch; there heartwood is revealed in sharp, wriggly waves, and highlights thin or swell like watered silk. This rich decoration makes wood more than just a handy neutral. You can retain the pattern and texture by adding colour in the form of stain rather than paint.

The grain of some woods is more picturesque than that of others; pine, oak and walnut are inspirationally figured. Grain may be straight, irregular or interlocked; texture coarse or fine; natural colour anywhere from the creamy white of balsa to the deep purple of rosewood or even ebony's jet black.

To apply a wood-grain finish, use a pale, oil-based eggshell background paint and a darker, transparent oil glaze. The oily medium is necessary because the main figuring has to be done fairly quickly, and oil glaze can be moved around before it sets hard. Whether you choose to stay with a natural coloration or cut loose with some juicier shades, the usual procedure is tone on tone, with the graining considerably deeper than the base, so that the former is thrown into relief. Professional grainers have special implements, but the amateur can get by with an assortment of brushes (some with bristles removed to create gaps) and fine-to-coarse combs – depending on the area to be tackled. For large areas, the grain itself is the thing to concentrate on – once the fine, flowing, gracefully curving lines of the grain have been captured, give the finish more character by adding details like knots and heart wood.

A bold wall treatment is the key to satisfying, original, coordinated schemes for each room. In this room the blue forms a link between the chill, modern – somewhat surreal – theatre poster and the gentle, folksy, floral blinds. It contrasts richly with the reds of the fabrics used on the sofa, extemporized from an old-fashioned cot. The rosy, plummy hues spring to life far more readily than if seen against pale, natural pine.

Blue-stained walls make an unpredictable and distinctly moody change from the usual plain pine in this cabin retreat. The textural interest provided by the grain is undiminished. The floor, window frames and carved pelmets have been left natural, keeping the balance between town and country, old and new, in this city-dwellers' weekend hideaway. The theme has been sustained throughout the house with each of the rooms stained a different and quite intense shade – pink, yellow, turquoise – with all the floors their original neutral hue.

A delicate jade-green effect combines both grain and stain to resemble pine which has been decoratively tinted. The technique is tone on tone, with the ground a paler version of the deeper graining glaze.

Such a natural pine finish could be given to papered or plastered walls, to inferior composite wood sheeting or even to the enamelled metal of appliances. Both natural and fantasy colours are suitable for cupboards,

closets, bath panels and built-in units, as well as walls. In addition to the traditional comb and brush methods, there are, on the market, small rollers specially designed to imitate wood grain.

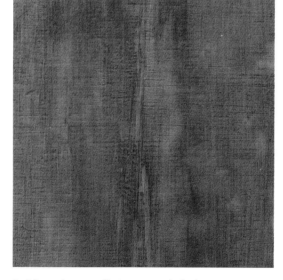

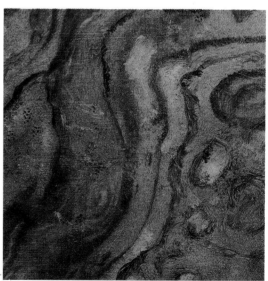

A rich, mahogany effect could be used in quantity to make a room look warmer and cosier. The brushwork runs in both directions, with the basic vertical grain applied sandwich-fashion. Fine horizontal striations in between produce the

interlocked grain, characteristic of certain mahoganies. Notice also that the background colour changes subtly in density, for greater realism.

A more dramatic look is obtained by imitating walnut. Real walnut is regarded as one of the world's favourite decorative woods for cabinet-work, or as a veneer for panelling or furniture. As a graining effect, walnut is highly figurative, and

requires a variety of smudging, stippling and varnishing procedures. It is difficult to apply to large areas, but is, in any case, more suited to accents like table-tops or doors.

ILLUSIONS OF MARBLE

Marble's unique, endlessly varied patterns and subtle-to-striking colours evoke the power and mystery of the earth's formation. It is one of our most naturally decorative raw materials and needs only to be cut and polished to reveal its timeless, majestic beauty. Since ancient times artists have been moved to imitate it for both aesthetic and practical reasons. When the real thing has been hard to come by, or when the look appeals even though the heavy stone would be unwieldy in context, *trompe-l'œil* marbling comes into its own.

Precise imitation of specific real marbles – pale travertine, veined breccia or fossil-studded crinoidal, for instance – recreating their original coloration, is one of the most disciplined painterly crafts. Close and continuing study of the genuine article is required to capture the eddying swirls, veins and nebular patterning, the illusion of depth and the evocation of antiquity. The samples shown here are the work of a specialist, but the amateur can get surprisingly impressive results using basic sponging, a spontaneous impressionistic technique and aiming simply for a fanciful effect.

Observe the marbles around you and study the techniques of marbling. Then – armed only with ordinary items like oil-based paint, fine sandpaper, a tiny brush, a sponge, varnish, french chalk, a soft polishing cloth and a good deal of patience – you can magically transform plain wood or plaster into ornamental stone.

Artificial marbling should emulate the natural, loose, random, unrepeated quality. This can, however, be manipulated to attract the eye to, or draw it away from, certain areas by varying the density of the pattern. The extensive range of natural colours, produced by impurities in the rock, may be infinitely augmented for the purposes of decorative marbling. Incorporate tones from the room scheme, for instance, or try a completely unlikely coloration for dramatic effect.

There are many potential applications for marbling: from accents, such as picture frames, to grander things such as whole floors. To gain confidence, start small on, say, a box, but think big. After all, you are interpreting a classic.

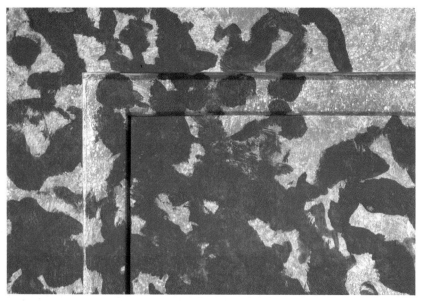

This startling, high contrast pattern may look unlikely close up, but it is an exact replica of marble used extensively in the palace of Versailles as it particularly suited the heroic scale of the interior. The effect is best viewed at a distance, lending itself well to baseboards, door frames or, perhaps, a table-top.

Painting over wood, the artist has prepared a blue-grey-white, grainy background (which at first glimpse one could easily take for granite) and superimposed the dramatic blood red which is characteristic of this type of French marble.

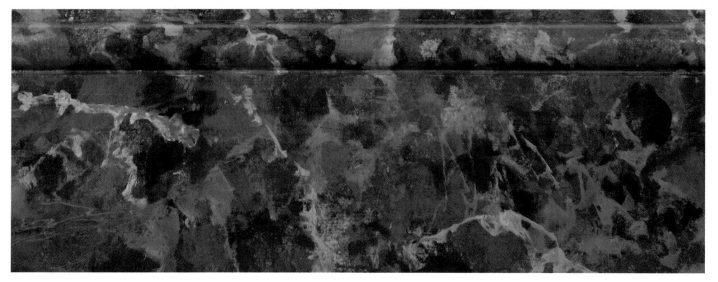

Rich tones of rust, mossy green and umber combine to reveal that marbling can appear warm and intimate as well as cool. This particular coloration, based on a marble called 'rouge royal' has a mellow, autumnal, masculine look. The dense pattern and deep colours applied, as here, to baseboards would suit a den or library. The closely-worked graining has strong visual interest and would give an ornamental lift to any room in need of a touch of class.

The glowing, honey-toned coloration of the wallpaper used in this bathroom has a warmer feel than real marble, but the pattern still captures the essence of the natural material. Such an airy, large-scale design is best where marbling is to be used in quantity. Ideally, the veining should appear random, avoiding any conspicuous area repeat. The marbled facing makes an attractive backdrop for the collection of luxurious bath accessories.

The marble look is perennially appropriate in bathrooms. It has a traditional association with fountains and splashing water and it lends a note of elegance to a purely functional room. Using light-coloured marbling on the walls of a small bathroom makes it seem more spacious, particularly if you also use it to camouflage the fittings. The effect can be achieved by several means – wallpaper, tiles or formica sheets – as well as paint.

The fantasy, seascape tones used on this section of moulding are an exaggeration of actual *verte de mer* (sea-green) marble colours, but they are so harmonious and appealing that the eye does not register a fake; it simply accepts the ingenious effect. The balance has been achieved by using variations of the same basic shade, from its darkest right through to almost pure white. Like the sea itself, or certain pairs of eyes, the colour emphasis shifts between grey, green and blue, according to the light and the context in which it is seen. Whether you intend to evoke genuine marble tones or simply adapt the pattern to your own colour scheme, a close and continuing study of real marble is invaluable.

STENCILLING

The technique of applying pattern to a surface through a cut-out of cardboard or acetate, is one most of us have been familiar with since childhood.

Happily, it is currently enjoying a revival in decorating. It not only gives artistic confidence and satisfaction, it has an especially homey, old-world quality, particularly appealing now that so many furnishings are mass-produced and characterless. Nevertheless, it can also look quite discreet and sophisticated; everything depends upon the constituent colours and shapes.

Stencils may be applied to any surface: walls, floors, woodwork and even furniture and soft furnishings. They can be used both to accentuate architectural features in handsomely proportioned rooms and to create interest in otherwise dull, box-like rooms.

You can buy ready-made stencils, or produce your own. Crafts supply shops sell tracing paper for drawing up the designs, specially-made waxed stencil paper or acetate (slightly harder to cut, but more durable if re-use is planned) and craft knives, scalpels or single-edge razors for the cutting out. There are traditional, stubby, stiff-bristled stencil brushes which can be used with a stippling motion, or you can simply use an ordinary small brush, pulling your strokes in towards the middle of the cut-out to prevent paint leaking under the stencil.

Work with paint of a fairly dry consistency and keep a small supply of the background colour handy for last minute tidying up.

An exquisite device of fruit with trailing leaves and ribbons is given extra dimension and modelling by relieving the usual flat finish of a stencil with touch-ups in various colours of spray paint over the base. A simplified version of this elaborate cut-out could be made up using three or four of the basic small shapes in a clever composition.

To produce this versatile geometric border pattern, three separate stencils are required – one for each colour. Clear acetate stencils are best as you can align separate sections more easily and acetate also wipes clean for re-use. Repeated to form a block this motif could – in the right colours – have an almost Art Deco look.
The twinkling stars are a motif which has been used since Egyptian times to adorn vaulted ceilings. Gold stencilled over azure is traditional, but the colours can be changed to suit the particular interior.
Both motifs are adapted from Owen Jones's *Grammar of Ornament*, the classic design reference.

Three completely different approaches to stencilling embellish this modernized, medieval tithe barn. The small chest in the corner combines several motifs to produce an exotic, tiger-toned, two-colour picture, with tawny orange stencilled over a deep brown ground. The filmy white curtain has a base-border floral decoration of delicately graded greens, pinks and beige – quite disparate in character from the dominant floor pattern. The strong Venetian-red and black, geometric motifs, make the wood floor look almost like a carpet, complete with distinctive chevron border. Needlework cushions complement the floor.

Such an appealing image can be applied in mural size, using one big stencil and masking off the appropriate areas as you apply each colour. To use it small, as a repeat, you need a separate stencil for each colour, with register marks in the corners so that they can be aligned.

On a white wall as stark as the Arctic, a row of penguins is a delightful sight. Cartoon-style animal motifs are always popular for children's rooms, and if they are sufficiently stylish, adults appreciate them equally.

Light-heartedness radiates from these airy, innocent patterns with their arbitrary proportions and whimsical colours – blue willows, pink urns, brown foliage. They are an example of how stencils allow you to suit colour and shape exactly to your decorating requirements. The ochre in the border matches the blind; the brown, the cork tiles, while the stencilled birds are echoed by the charming wooden ones.

The total look is reminiscent of Eastern European or Alpine folk art, and it points up the special homey quality – the human touch – that stencilling so readily provides in town as well as country settings.

COLLAGE

Collage is a wonderfully free-wheeling art form, requiring neither paint nor special graphic skill. We can use it to display our memories, collections, whims and individuality. Strictly speaking, it is a composition of materials and objects pasted over a surface, often with unifying lines and/or colour imposing a discreet order. For inspiration, get familiar with the range of this medium – from the simple, charming paper cut-outs of Henri Matisse to the outlandish conglomerations of Robert Rauschenberg.

Collage offers the decorator a chance to accentuate the personal with cheap, fast, original, fun wall coverings or focal points. You can get more mileage out of items you already own, as well as making the most of countless inexpensive materials. Everyday ephemera, massed according to a theme of colour, shape or subject, take on a fascinating organic structure.

Magazine covers and cut-outs, posters, post cards, photographs, marbled book endpapers, gift wrap, commercial envelopes – any interesting image or object – can be part of your masterpiece, so get pasting.

An assortment of relatively inexpensive embroidered Indian squares has been sewn edge to edge to create a rich wall hanging. Because each square has a pattern worthy of display, the only overlapping occurs at the bottom, to even it up.

Variations on this theme can be worked using any type of fabric items, such as silk or cotton scarves. If you do not want to sew them together, simply pin them in place. Squares can give a more dynamic look when turned to form diamond shapes. Fabric collages may be further unified by scattering a repeating, cut-out motif over them – or just a spray of glitter or some small stick-on stars.

A stylish mantelpiece backdrop has been created by giving this picture collage a bias toward blue. The hue knits the images together and acts as a foil for the elegant dark-stain finish on both shelf and clock. It is given a symmetry by repetition of certain images. Centred toward the bottom, the large, familiar photograph of the Pharaoh Tutankhamun's gold-and-lapis-lazuli funeral mask anchors and dominates the pattern. It is 'framed' by cats – Ancient Egypt's most revered creatures – whose pictures are arranged in a pyramid shape. Random cut-out Egyptian motifs further embellish the composition. Collage is an ideal medium for fun with private symbolism.

The mixing of two- and three-dimensional decoration is obvious at shelf level, but more subtle elsewhere – the greatly magnified watch face in the photograph ironically dwarfs the real clock on the mantelpiece.

A protective coat of varnish would enrich the colour and further unify the collage by giving it a more finished look.

The juxtaposition of images old and new, familiar and enigmatic, painted and photographed, imbues the collage with a sense of activity and interest. It is naturally idiosyncratic, but linking themes – both of colour and subject – make it strong and positive.

Multi-coloured sheets of ordinary stationery or coloured paper overlap to produce a surprisingly stylish effect. The pieces are stuck down in a random patchwork pattern, rather than a regimented check, creating an interesting tension. Each is seen against all the other colours in a variety of proportions; the result is a happy balance. Using this technique in a more calculated manner, it would be possible to build toward a band of solid colour at a border, or even create a 'frame' for the painting.

A high-spirited collection of ties comes out of the closet to become a personal work of art. Displayed hanging over three tiers of wire, they remain ready to wear and fun to select. As a collage, they are unified by shape and texture, and by a coloration weighted toward the primaries.

The geometric motif is echoed imaginatively in the décor. The table of mirror squares reflects both the wall collage and the Deco-style painting, to warm and enliven an interior otherwise cooled by pastel and gleam. Similarly, the mirrored folding screen makes a mosaic of whatever it happens to reflect.

135

Colour styles

How do painters, designers, architects – people whose livelihood is bound up with colour – decorate their own homes? Every bit as individually as they sign their names!

They dispense with commercial formulae and traditional rules, expressing themselves so emphatically that most have furnishings custom-made to suit their schemes. Often their choices are intuitive, and if you find the courage to develop ideas this way, your home will benefit from genuine originality and appear natural rather than forced.

We examine a dozen fascinating interiors from all over the world and discover that, even for those who do it professionally, living with colour means entirely different things to different people.

Location is a factor, but not the most important: Le Corbusier in France and Luis Barragan in Mexico, for instance, have more in common than do Tricia Guild and Duggie Fields, who live ten minutes apart in central London. Architects often use colour to celebrate their passion for light and form, and to realize their mission to provide tranquillity in an increasingly graceless world. Artists and designers make colour the key to self-expression, so that their homes are organically related to their work – both a showcase for past creations and a matrix for future style. They know from experience how important it is to take charge of their surroundings, since they are continually affected by them.

Use the following interiors to discover what you respond to – both positively and negatively. They are presented not as models to be copied, but rather to show widely varied approaches to the handling of colour's power. Although dramatically diverse in appearance, they are unified by the spirit of experimentation and insight into colour's magic.

The author created a holiday atmosphere in a home he once had in the London suburbs by using a fresh contrast of cherry-blossom-pink upholstery with turquoise walls to make the most of the light and foliage overflowing from the conservatory.

DUNCAN GRANT

The painter and decorative artist, Duncan Grant, was a key figure in what came to be called the Bloomsbury Group. This diversely talented set of intellectual renegades, the most famous of whom was novelist Virginia Woolf, lived a loosely communal life in London and the Sussex countryside in the opening decades of the century. As a pacifist, Grant was obliged to do agricultural work during the First World War. His painting partner, Vanessa Bell, found the farmhouse called Charleston which became home for her own family, as well as Grant and writer David Garnett. The entire interior – walls, windows, furniture, fabrics, crockery – was treated as one great canvas, tirelessly embellished by the inhabitants with paint, stencilling and glaze. It was neither posh nor a vehicle for rebel chic. It was simply jubilant, independent expression – laughter made graphic.

In the course of time, the others died or moved, while Grant remained and Charleston became a *de facto* monument to his charmingly animated, gaily coloured and perpetually youthful style.

Taste was never an issue at Charleston. The entire spirit of the Bloomsbury Group in their rural exile, as in London, was to express themselves intuitively, neither courting approval nor indulging in deliberate iconoclasm. There is no anger in this decoration, no belligerent flaunting of rules; just a comfy, supremely relaxed – and at the same time, creatively energetic – enjoyment of colour and shape. It is imbued with the light-heartedness of true freedom. It is messy, by conventional standards, but it is *their* mess, and it certainly cannot be accused of taking itself seriously. As the studio in a house where painting never stopped, this room is entitled to its air of artless *déshabillé*.

Muted versions of the primaries, compatible with their warm, neutral background, are applied in a folk-art pattern to the window surround. Duncan Grant had a way with blobs – 'radiant doodling' it has been called – that elevated them to the sublime. The confident, rhythmic flair of his brushwork rendered such naive patterns as identifiably his as a signature.

An outsize vase and happy flowers, set in a make-believe alcove, adorn the reveal. Grant believed cheerfully in ornament for its own sake – a decorative philosophy repudiated by those who maintain that function is beauty, but one embraced by all who share a childlike appreciation of surfaces dressed up.

The bust fits well here, with its matching colours and innocent look.

The whimsical spirit of the interior is apparent in this fireplace surround where two robust youths have been painted to resemble casual statues – less interested in supporting the mantelpiece than leaning on a table dominated by a most unlikely-looking goldfish bowl. The bright colours are those associated with the Fauvist (from the French for 'wild beast') art movement, but are tempered by Grant's lightness and grace.

The tiles behind the stove and at its foot, at child's eye level, are decorated in colours and patterns that a child might choose. Quentin Bell, recalling his early years at Charleston, says the floor was frequently covered in tempting jars and saucers of paint, and that the happiness the grown-ups found in their liberal use of colour was communicated to the young.

The dark walls, roughly painted like a prepared canvas, are framed in a lighter shade, giving definition to the different panels of wall space.

The frieze above the mantel incorporates two self-framed still lifes, flanking a *trompe-l'œil* niche for the Buddha. The colours link it to the fireplace surround below.

The lampshade and double-handled pot, as well as the painted chest beneath, are reminders that Grant and his cronies painted everything that would take paint. He made his name as a decorative artist at the same time as he was evolving as a painter. The spirited attack on fabric, ceramic and wood evokes his 1913 to 1919 stint with the Omega Workshops, where young artists were employed to make and decorate a wide range of household objects. The use of line and colour suggests one of the mentors of his emerging years. Matisse.

The outrageous cloth draped over the sagging armchair is a great, hooting blast of new colour in a room which had been occupied by Grant for more than half a century. It is nothing more than colour in its own right, bizarre, almost molecular, forming the ultimate contrast laid against an honourably shabby, traditional floral print.

The huge, pillar-like lamp base is painted to echo the curtain and bedspread. The soft, earthy coloration is more typical of the rest of the living quarters of the house than is the flamboyant hodgepodge of the studio.

Paint patterns every surface – wood, plaster, cloth, ceramic – in this bedroom corner. The circles and the arched shape of the little floor-level alcoves are motifs employed throughout the house.

LUIS BARRAGAN

A place out of the sun is the possibly controversial object of Luis Barragan's designs. He looks to colour rather than light for brilliance. The Mexican architect grew up with a deep appreciation of the rugged natural beauty and formidable extremes of his native land. His childhood vacations were spent exploring mountains and lush valleys accessible only on horseback, and his adult career has been distinguished by the attempt to preserve that same spiritual privacy in over-populated urban settings. He has worked to counteract those buildings styles he deplores as belittling both humanity and architecture. 'About half the glass that is used in so many buildings – homes as well as offices – would have to be removed in order to obtain the quality of light that enables one to live and work in a more concentrated manner, and more graciously.' With influences ranging from Mexico's Aztec heritage to Le Corbusier, whose lectures he attended in Paris, he evolved a style to celebrate the contemplative inner life, from which source true peace of mind may possibly be generated.

'**All of architecture** which does not express serenity fails in its spiritual mission. Thus it has been a mistake to abandon the shelter of walls for the inclemency of large areas of glass' argues Barragan, who favours quiet, enclosures where solitude and thought are possible.

The careful placement of hefty blocks of primary colour with a powerful sculptural function is a hallmark of Luis Barragan's work. He systematically uses colour as an integral part of his structures, to emphasize form and react with the changing light. Although this is, in fact, a small house, the unadorned planes of the walls make the feeling of space paradoxically generous. The bright hues make up for the fact that there is no other artwork to appease the eye. They themselves form a composition not unlike a single, enormous modern abstract painting.

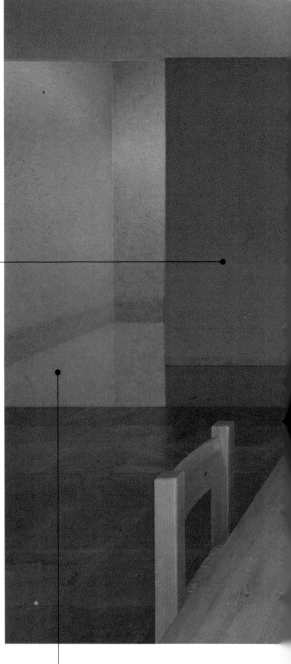

From a precisely positioned aperture, a laser-sharp shaft of sunlight, as bright as white paint, pierces the still, cool atmosphere. It enhances the already strongly sculptural quality of this watery corner, its angle subtly altering with the changing light. The acute contrast with the gently dim interior reinforces Barragan's plea for our need of half-light, 'We should try to recover mental and spiritual ease . . . the pleasures of thinking, working, conversing are heightened by the absence of glaring, distracting light.'

Water is an element of surprise used in this way. It contributes both to Barragan's efforts to establish peace in his interiors, and to his fascination with the effects of shifting natural light, which changes the surface colour continually.

Natural materials – the stone floor and wood furniture – glory in their plain lines, neutral tones and solid textures. They do nothing to detract from the prevailing calm, while the heaped fruit is a riot of plenty in the midst of such total austerity.

'The large wall surfaces reflect varying luminosity, which in turn creates a comfortable, intimate atmosphere,' says Barragan, who has devised ingenious methods of modulating the harsh Mexican sun, so that his interiors have the tranquil air of a sanctuary.

The red door has been hinged so as to swing back flat against the wall, and it is hung a step up from floor level, so that when it is open, as here, it forms a symmetrical, two-panel mural-like composition.

VALENTINO

Fashion designer Valentino has remained faithful, both privately and professionally, to his native Rome. Although Milan is now regarded as the capital of Italian couture, he makes the Eternal City his home and the heart of his international business empire.

His lavish villa near the Appian Way has a traditional appearance outside, but the interior is by no means a predictable show-place of contemporary Italian design. Rather, in the eclectic spirit of Ancient Rome, it is a glorious monument to his world travels and his personal taste.

There is a deliberate dichotomy within the house, distinguishing the immaculate stately rooms where he entertains from the colourful private apartments where a degree of comfortable disorder is allowed. In the former, a good deal of classic white prevails, evocative of the 1967 collection which brought Valentino to prominence; in the latter, shades, rich as the ochre-red roof-tops of Rome, create the inviting atmosphere he so values. His ruling passion is for beautiful things: he has filled the house with artistic treasures from his extensive globe trotting. Surfaces and objects have been orchestrated in a manner that is flamboyant but controlled, to reproduce a live-in Valentino original.

Valentino collaborated with two interior designers – one for the elegant public rooms and one for his private living quarters – when making over his Roman villa. The contrasting styles are represented by this cosy Victorian salon with a view into the spacious, formal living room.

White is a perennial favourite with Valentino. Here it provides a timeless context in which a Picasso floats amidst massive, Egyptian-inspired columns. The white scheme was also selected to set off the lush garden greenery lying just beyond.

Matching flowered chintz covers the walls and sofa of this compact Victorian salon, the deep colours and bold pattern drawing the little room together. An ormolu chandelier casts an amber glow over the armchair. adorned with *petit point* embroidery and lace. The large Botero painting is modern, but with its plump family and warm coloration. suits the snug theme.

Printed cotton with a large paisley motif covers the walls and is gathered into two great, floor-length curtains for an inviting, almost tented, look. The motif recurs, in a warmer, spice-toned version, on the bedspread.

The two Ching dynasty portraits are of a Manchu prince and his consort. Their majestic proportions suit the opulence of the furnishings, while their dramatic scarlets and blacks are echoed in accents all around the room.

Luxurious furs in ginger and cinnamon shades on the Empire bed, reading-chair and antique, Italian *chaise longue* romantically enhance the Eastern, nomadic spirit of the room.

Light bounces between the
gleaming marble floor and
gloss white ceiling,
magnifying the already
generous space. The
ambience is serene, sublime
and sophisticated.

A large potted palm
softens lines, gives another
dimension of green, and
echoes the shrubs in the
paper pattern.

Valentino's passion for
Chinese statuary is indulged
with this imposing mandarin
and a pair of splendid T'ang
dynasty horses. The rich
hues of the mandarin's
flowing robes are repeated
in the horses' elaborate
trappings.

Antique Persian carpets
are displayed to advantage
on the pale, shining floor.
Their discreetly faded tones
are complemented by the
subtle neutrals of the fossil-
marble table.

The painted paper on the
gallery walls creates a
tapestry effect. This jade-
green and rose-pink oriental
design was reproduced from
a paper discovered on the
walls in an old villa.

ERIC JACOBSON

A haven apart from the stress and stridency of twentieth-century living – that is Eric Jacobson's working ideal.

The Swedish-born interior designer, now long resident in West Germany, is best known for schemes he describes as 'no-colour'. Inevitably some degree of colour is pesent, but it is so skilfully controlled, so systematically reduced, that the impact is of dream-like unreality. Nowhere in nature would one find the mysterious, monochrome quality displayed here in his elegant, turn-of-the-century Hamburg apartment.

Jacobson claims that he is neither a German nor a Swedish designer. He describes himself as European, and holds good design is international. He encourages personal identity; he is dismissive of design that is conspicuously nationalistic. He is equally reluctant to tie himself artistically to a specific period. Because of his early training, he used antiques extensively when he started in interiors. He has now, however, relegated them to the rank of accessories.

He believes that no single design style can evoke the total serenity he seeks on behalf of his clients. A pure period approach – Louis-Seize or Empire, for instance – he finds overpowering, like walking into a museum. 'Anyone with enough money can do that. It's not a question of design or taste.' Nor is he sold on the virtues of high-tech, although he finds it exciting. He feels it makes too many demands on those who live with it.

His solution lies in a selectivity which emphasizes works of art, light and texture. Glass, crystal, silver, gilt, acres of white and honeyed neutrals share a hushed dynamic range, a harmonious peace that lasts. 'I'd never do anything that would tire quickly.'

The vaulted false ceiling contributes an intimate, canopy effect to this otherwise stark space. Light filters from its edges so that it appears to float, like a lid gently lifting from the walls of matching honey tone.

The large, glazed panel with its inset door maximizes the available light and averts any possibility of claustrophobia in this dining area, reclaimed from what was originally closet space.

The large, almost empty, canvas perfectly expressing Jacobson's no-colour minimalism, is all but absorbed into the background. The tiny spoon and glass link it to its dining-room setting. The square format echoes the wall on which it hangs – the wall itself delicately framed with narrow moulding as if it, too, were a painting.

The sleek, almost bare, marble table has a strong, sculptural look. Its altar-like quality is enhanced by candles, whose clear glass sticks are a calculated accent in the no-colour theme.

The pale, shiny floor of light-reflecting tiles completes the walk-on-air, other-worldliness of this unusual space.

The paintings, which are the *raison d'être*, of this interior are seen in the context which best allows Jacobson to meditate on their content and beauty. Their diversity is unified by a common blue-grey tint.

The high ceilings have been painted white. This both lifts them and gives due attention to the room's majestic proportions and superlative mouldings, the hallmarks of traditional architectural quality.

The living-room walls have been given a slightly rough texture akin to parchment. It lends them greater visual interest while adding warmth to the lighting. Their unobtrusive tone is ideal as a backdrop for paintings.

The close-fitted carpet has been chosen carefully as an almost identical colour match with the walls. That, and the similarity of texture combine to accentuate the illusion of a free-floating cell in no-colour-land.

Lighting is crucial to the ethereal atmosphere. The transparent-base lamp with gilded shade, the sofa back-lighting and the burning tapers, together create the strange, candle-light colour that suffuses this space.

The sofa and armchair upholstery is the epitome of chromatic restraint. It blends passively with its surroundings, yet subtly different textures have been achieved with fine striped or trellised weaves.

ZANDRA RHODES

With her unique command of colour and line, Zandra Rhodes is a design phenomenon. Her clothes come close to being tangible fantasies, and brave new fashion ideas sizzle non-stop up through her fuschia-pink hair. She lives for her work, and the London house she describes as her 'second skin' is both a monument to her provocative style and a matrix for future creations. She is, first and always, a fabric designer. From this evolved the fashions made exclusively from her own materials, as well as a range of furnishing textiles, wallpapers and ceramic tiles. The ruffles, shine and wriggly lines that make her dresses instantly identifiable are an integral part of all aspects of her interior decoration.

Zandra Rhodes originals have bedecked Jackie Onassis, Diana Ross and New York's Metropolitan Museum of Art. They appeal to the conventional and the outrageous alike. The same Zandra who designed Princess Anne's engagement dress was subsequently dubbed 'Queen of Punk' for her *haute couture* interpretation of the slashes-and-safety-pins trend. She simply keeps an open mind and works intuitively.

When it comes to her own home, she believes in surrounding herself with things she loves so that it always gives her morale a boost. Designers must be continually refreshed and refuelled for further efforts. She makes no distinction between her colour use for interiors and that for clothes. 'As you can see, a lot of the stuff in my own home was what was left over from my dress fabrics. I just use whatever comes along in whatever way seems to work in a particular situation.'

The basement conversion shown here makes ingenious use of a confined space. The amber-gleaming bathroom was reclaimed from a former wine cellar; the bedroom is literally a glorified bed, and prized by Zandra for its proximity to her beloved garden.

Glamour, femininity and a quality of pure escapism characterize all her work. With regard to interiors she sums up, 'Surfaces are the thing,' and hers are liberally endowed with sparkle, frills and the pinky-peachy hues she adores. As well as her magical fabrics, attention to detail marks her success in both fashion and decorating. As she says, 'My whole life is one big design.'

The dark disk shining above the bed has been painted to suggest a romantic, limitless night sky, alive with shooting stars.

The fantasy quality of the room is derived largely from the masses of exquisite printed tulle draping the walls. The fine, filmy fabric was one Zandra designed for evening dresses. The wall shown here has gold lurex hung behind the almost transparent net; on other walls it is backed by pink mosaic mirror, giving a dreamy, fleeting reflection.

The plain, cream-coloured lamp discreetly reinforces the Zandra Rhodes look with its pleated shade and softly swirled base.

A generous floor-to-ceiling mirror maximizes the sense of space in this *bijou* bathroom, while doubling up the jewel-like sparkle of every shiny surface.

Zandra's designing hand is apparent in the wriggly-patterned tiles and the mirror, engraved with one of her free-form 'faces' – here like a cloud teeming wavy rain-like lines.

The lustrous, bronze-fleck fixtures, with towels in matching tones, look both warm and opulent.

Gold scintillates from the fine, mosaic tile floor and the fittings – chosen as much for their colouring as for their deliberate luxury.

The bed cushions have an exuberant Hollywood glamour about them – the wiggly lines leaping like party streamers against champagne-pink satin, while silvery, fluted ruffles heighten the luscious frivolity. All are Zandra's own designs, as is the bedspread in subtle tones of lavender, peach and terracotta.

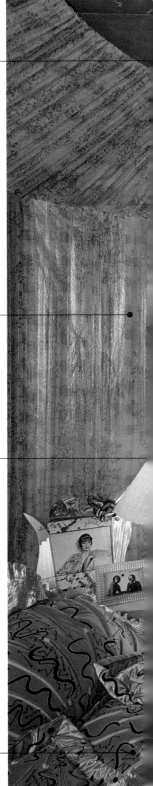

This delicious heap of cushions embodies a recent Zandra Rhodes fabric collection, creating a display with considerably more verve than simple swatches. Characteristic ruffles and wriggles abound as the same patterns recur in assorted colour-ways. The colours generally are her perennial favourites – if anything, she feels, a bit richer than usual.

The Zandra Rhodes whimsy at full throttle is typified by this blackamoor – originally a white, Greek-style plaster model, extravagantly made over with paint and draped in some of her fabric.

The glazed door opens on to a private, city garden so beloved by the owner that she likes to be able to see out to it from the comfort of her bed.

The undulating shelf was built to Zandra's specifications – giving her wavy-line hallmark three-dimensional form.

The mock columns are made from the hefty paper cores on which bulk fabric is delivered. Four have been used in all, adorned with the signature wiggle in gloss black. The idea was to evoke the feeling that this tiny room is really just a giant four-poster bed, in a garden under the night sky.

LE CORBUSIER

The grandfather of high-tech, the maestro of concrete, Swiss-born Charles-Edouard Jeanneret changed his name to Le Corbusier and changed the look of architecture in the twentieth century. He built his first house when not yet 18 years old; it was radical, risk-taking, revolutionary. The man who was to describe himself as 'an impenitent visionary' spent a lifetime rapt with the potential of the new mechanized society and with the possibilities that architecture held for optimizing the quality of life.

The rather disproportionately well-known comment made by Le Corbusier with regard to domestic building design was that a house should be 'a machine for living in'. In fact, he felt just as passionately about the spiritual as the practical responsibilities of housing. Reflecting late in life he said, 'I have for fifty years been studying this chap known as "Man" and his wife and kids. I have been inspired by one single preoccupation, imperatively so: to introduce into the home the sense of the sacred; to make the home the temple of the family'. This resolve produced interiors that still appear daring and uncompromising, over half a century later. He exhibits the architect's trait of avoiding pattern to concentrate the eye on form. His use of colour is heroic and informed with mathematical precision and grace.

Le Corbusier, a contemporary of the Cubist painters and the Bauhaus designers, was a 'form-follows-function' adherent, and his geometric, abstract, lyrically sculptural work straddled the scientific and the artistic cultures.

The hand of Le Corbusier is unmistakable in these two villas, both with dramatic integral lines which distinguish them from traditional interiors and which reveal their creator as sculptor, painter, and even poet, as well as formidable architect. The La Roche house at Auteuil, with its streamlined ramp, and the Villa Savoye at Poissy, with its undulating tiled 'chaise', illustrate Le Corbusier's dictum: 'Architecture is the skilful, correct and magnificent play of shapes assembled in the light.'

Chrome columns, table legs and armchair supports add a welcome, enlivening sparkle throughout.

Planes, rather than patterns, are featured in this largely achromatic plan. The black square of floor echoes the black table; the horizontal shelf above the radiator is picked out, while the radiator itself is all but camouflaged. Even the black armchairs have flush lines.

The stunning diagonal sweep of the stair ramp gives life and movement to this entire space. It creates the sensation of soaring up to the light – a light which, because it is streaming in from above, makes the area below feel particularly private. The deep grey band has, in addition to its exceptional structural quality, a role as the middle tone in a scheme which concentrates areas of black at the base and an expanse of white at the top.

This alcove, treated as a three-dimensional painting, makes a striking, warm focal point in such an austere context. The scarlet panel glows in its frame of umber, red-ochre and black.

Muted blue tiles subtly isolate a step-up, sunken bath area, designed in strict right angles like the tiles themselves. Blue also defines the middle level between floor and 'chaise'.

White floor-to-ceiling tiles, ceramic fixtures and painted columns, woodwork and radiator help to illuminate this confined space. Natural and artificial lighting play up white's sculptural values.

The highly original, built-in *chaise longue* is a design Le Corbusier pioneered. A dark band highlights its curving lines, while its sandy-beige tiles tone with the larger floor tiles.

OLIVER MESSEL

Sweet were the uses of adversity for theatrical designer and architect, Oliver Messel. Arthritis struck him when his international career was still flourishing, and, to the dismay of his many friends, he decided to accomodate his health by moving from London to warmer climes.

The notion of constructing a West Indies homestead from scratch in Barbados had long appealed to him. For several years prior to his permanent move, he assiduously bought up the tiny, adjoining parcels of land at Mango Bay which now comprise the estate called Maddox.

Work began on the old plantation house in 1968 and was completed the next year, expedited by Messel's combined talents, one of which was to give Maddox a convincing antique finish, as if it had been in his family for generations. He had effected sweeping reforms, reorienting the structure to accentuate glorious gardens reclaimed from lamentable dereliction. 'I reversed everything.' He put in a courtyard, built loggias and balconies, added a garden room and opened the dining- and living-rooms at the sides. A colonnaded passage running right through the house exploits the light and creates perspectives.

The attention to detail that distinguished his theatrical work – from Noël Coward revues to the Royal Ballet – was evident in Maddox's many custom-designed furnishings – from table legs to lamp brackets – which are Messel originals.

Messel's use of white recalls the early days of his career, around 1930, when he was instrumental in launching the vogue for white interiors, featuring colour in flowers or accessories. Here it reflects his sensitivity to and reverence for his adopted paradise. A true professional, he had better sense than to try to upstage Nature. Rather, he enjoyed the spectacle from the best seats in the house.

A mixture of influences – traditional European, theatrical, original Messel and pure Nature – blend harmoniously.

Radiant white walls of local coral stone are the perfect foil for the abundant greenery inside and out.

The elaborate, wrought-iron dining-table stand, with its scrolled feet and flourishing acanthus leaves all painted a deep, gloss green, was designed by Messel. It supports a green-veined, Italian *antiqua verde* marble top brought out from England. The combined effect is original Messel – more colourful than ordinary local furniture, yet completely and immediately in keeping with its surroundings.

The wide, white floor is another triumphant Messel invention. It is a mixture of coral and cement, glazed with varnish to produce the mellow patina of marble. Diamonds of genuine green marble were used for the jewel-like insets. The floor's coloration is an exquisitely judged match with the table top, and literally the ideal foundation for this airy, green-and-white room scheme.

Even the foliage has been carefully selected to echo the green-and-white theme in the most natural way.

The exceedingly ornate, gilded frame evokes Messel's years as a theatrical set and furniture designer.

Uniform white coral stone walls let the eye travel unimpeded to discover a second colonnade opening the house to the left and a distant doorway beyond that.

The indoor/outdoor character of Maddox is concentrated in this loggia. The cosy, European sofa upholstered in classic blue-and-white *toile de jouy* looks out to a luxuriant garden beyond the colonnade.

Graceful arcades and colonnades created by architect/designer Messel are used extensively to allow the spectacular scenery – sea, sky and exotic gardens – to be admired from countless comfortable vantage points. As classic architectural shapes – and ones frequently employed by Messel on stage – they have an intrinsic, spirit-lifting quality that is further enhanced by their felicitous location.

The blue-and-white delf china, and the chair cushions in similar tones, represent traditional European design.

The multi-hued marble table-top provides a subtle colour transition between the floor and the delf china.

Mildew is less than a calamity in this context; its colour and texture fits in plausibly with both the arrangement of antiques and the décor as a whole.

The seashells and crystal-lined rocks are Nature's handiwork, as is the foliage beyond, glowing with near fluorescent intensity.

The pineapple-shaped table legs and richly varnished cement floor are Messel's own designs, inspired by their setting.

CLAUDE MONET

Claude Monet's delightful house at Giverny, the painter's home for the second half of his life, was, in many ways, the family seat of Impressionism. The house, which stands in the part of the village known as Le Pressoir – site of an ancient cider press – was found by Monet after a scrupulous, systematic search for a place with the elusive qualities of light he desired, illuminating wild, dense and abundant Normandy countryside.

A simple, informal lifestyle prevailed at Giverny, although the household did adhere to a fairly strict timetable, especially with regard to mealtimes, governed by Monet's self-imposed work routine. His great passion, apart from painting – although, in fact, inextricably linked – was his garden. It was here that his legendary water-lilies thrived beneath the bridge that was inspired by a favourite Japanese print.

Monet lived at Giverny for seven years before, at the age of fifty, finally buying the house. By then he was mature, secure and celebrated. The colour choices he made for each of the interiors are those of a great artistic genius at the height of his creative powers.

Monet's bathed-in-yellow dining-room brings to brilliant life the psychological theory that yellow is the happiest colour in the spectrum. Although Monet pre-dates the theory, his intuitive mastery of colour led him to use yellow in a room of key importance to him as gourmet, family man and host. Positive, dazzling-yet-liveable, it radiates what the French call *bien-être*, an unmistakable sense of well-being.

A sun-bright shade of yellow envelopes walls, woodwork and ceiling, while mouldings are highlighted in a subtly deeper tone. The look is hardly controversial by modern standards, but it was certainly a departure from the conventional decoration of his day.

Monet had two dinner services – dark blue for everyday and yellow Limoges, made to match the walls.

The delf plates on display, together with the fireplace tiles, make a crisp, blue-and-white accent and link the room with the kitchen.

The gleaming, green-glazed pottery picks out tones in the prints and is the spectral link between the blues and yellows.

The kitchen's almost palpably blue air recalls a remark by Delacroix, whose journals were among Monet's favourite regular bedside reading:
'When we look at ordinary, everyday objects which we see around us in a landscape or within a house, we cannot escape the fact that the atmosphere acts as a link between such objects, and that reflected light is the agent binding all things harmoniously together.'

Monet was so keen to keep his favourite cook happy that when she married he hired her husband as butler rather than lose her. He also made the kitchen environment as pleasing as possible.

Checks and tile patterns are combined with amicable spontaneity to give a cheerful, unpretentious working atmosphere.

The use of blue also has the practical advantage of making the room feel cool.

Monet was cited as 'the first painter genuinely to dispense with a focal point' – a trait which crops up in his decorating as well.

The all-over patterning in this room does not lead the eye, but lets it drift, surrounded by numerous impressions of blue.

The particular magic of a monochrome scheme may be seen in this patchwork of blues, assembled from a range of dark, medium and light tones.

Honey, blue and white checked gingham curtains with ruffles and tie-backs add a welcome, feminine touch to the room.

The riotous garden was Monet's pride, joy and inspiration throughout the forty-three years he was master of the house.

The tiles freely counterchange dark on light with light on dark in the random panel behind the stove.

The glittering utensils, adorning shelves and walls, were not just for show, as now; they were in constant use, their beauty a bonus.

153

TRICIA GUILD

Tricia Guild has perfected the art of making colour the medium for comfort. Her fabrics and interior designs are unabashedly pretty. The style of her company, Designers Guild, is readily recognizable, characterized by gentle tones, multiplicity of pattern and softened lines. Pastels, flowers and plants, grouped with a tantalizing trace of gypsy abandon, create a happy pot-pourri.

Tricia Guild describes the look in terms of mix, atmosphere and colour balance. She explains her preference for whitened colour levels as opposed to strong primaries: 'I find that I want to live in an atmosphere that I can change quickly, adding or taking away strong colour in the form of flowers, for instance.' With pastels as constants and brights as variables, the atmosphere is serene and undemanding.

Her penchant for pastels is founded on their infinite flexibility – the fact that no matter what colour an interior is based on, it can accommodate any combination of other tints, so long as their values are consistent. This same homogeneity of tone makes it easy for her to mix patterns – large and small, floral and geometric. Her choices are motivated also by sheer love of light. 'I love being outside; that freshness is what I try to capture.'

A town girl with a country spirit, she finds inspiration in the unique energy of spring, and has always needed at least a patch of garden to call her very own.

In her decorative approach there is a sense of benign crowding which makes people feel secure. The coloration is such that no matter how many ingredients are involved, the effect is never oppressive or claustrophobic. Surfaces are draped, shrouded, softened. The atmosphere is protective, uninsistent, generally feminine – although it adapts handily for men by emphasizing neutrals, geometrics and the sharp tang of deep green, glossy foliage. Either way, a Tricia Guild interior is a study in frondly persuasion.

Delicately mottled, pale rose fabric of a tone in tune with the upholstery pattern covers the walls in a sweetened neutral.

The quiet colours, soft texture and homely subject-matter of this picture – brown and white eggs on a china plate – set values for the room as a whole. Painter/designer Kaffe Fassett is one of the key influences on Tricia Guild's uninsistent style.

The predominantly geometric patterns of sofa and cushion show the pleasing flexibility of pastels in contexts other than floral.

The close pattern of the wall covering is loosened somewhat by the broadly scattered larger motifs. The effect is ideal as a backdrop in a room where mixed patterns are the theme.

This painting by Kaffe Fassett – a treasure trove of seashells spread out on a bright handkerchief lying on a piece of floral print – has vivid pink accents which are echoed in the porcelain lamp base and adjacent bowl, as well as by details in the cushion covers.

The chest was hand-painted by Kaffe Fassett in a shell-studded style, using colours sympathetic to the various fabrics present.

The woven blanket cascading gently to the floor, and the two tiers of cloth – a pale floral with a deeper-toned, long 'skirt' – draped over the table are trademark Guild devices for softening a room's lines.

Fabric covers the coffee table, unifying it with the rest of the furniture. The 'beany' print gives a mosaic or terrazzo effect.

The large still life, painted by Lillian Delevoryas, was an inspiration for the Tricia Guild collection called simply 'Watercolour' – a range which captures that medium's elusive magic.

Real flowers, potted or cut, are used extravagantly in all Tricia Guild schemes. She values them as strong colour accents which can be varied at will, while the trailing foliage contributes to a fresh, naturally casual atmosphere.

The translucent, jade-green glass vase is a happy colour match for the Victorian floral fireplace tiles, whose reedy-gold borders, in turn, link up well with the floor covering.

The wicker chair and baskets and the rush matting provide warm, textured neutrals with universal appeal. Tricia Guild enjoys wicker furniture for its comfort – the unpretentious, easeful creak.

YUTAKA IZUE

The impact of an interior created by architect and designer Yutaka Izue is simultaneously classic and futuristic. His provocative adaptation of traditional style hinges on original use of colour and line. He successfully gives rein to personal expression without in any way diminishing the spiritual, meditative qualities for which Japanese interiors are renowned.

Many standard features of Japanese housing developed historically, according to religious, governmental and geographical dictates. If they engendered nobility of spirit through restraint, they now provide an environmental antidote to the pressures of high-density living and the stress of competitive urban culture. Where the world becomes unbearably crowded and strident outside, the need increases for a sense of space, privacy and calm inside. The home should be a place of communion with art and Nature, a well-spring of inner tranquillity.

From a strict, formal and ritualized social order evolved simple structures, emphasizing natural materials and their neutral tones.

Movable walls, or *shāji*, reveal immaculate gardens; and the discreet, altar-like recess, called the *tokonoma*, is used to display a painting, ceramic work or flower arrangement. Beauty of proportion defines both the rooms and their few, carefully chosen, contents.

Yutaka Izue did not set out to design Kansai-style buildings, but he feels he was inevitably influenced by having been brought up in that district – which is also the home of many of his clients. He traces the Kansai presence in his work to the highly religious atmosphere of Kyoto, the city where he was raised, although he has been based in Osaka now for many years.

Izue has not compromised or Westernized his design heritage; rather, he has enriched it. His glowing, soulful interiors are the visual equivalent of a familiar melody subtly transposed to an exciting new key.

Fine strips of natural light illuminate the room from high above, giving the impression that the ceiling is floating – a classic Japanese visual device. Formerly, friezes of lattice-work were usual at this level for ventilation.

A deep orange glow alters the traditional image of the *tokonoma* recess. It retains its historic function as an area in which to display a solitary beautiful object – here a vase glazed in the room's two colours – but the unaccustomed strength of hue brings it forward into the modern world. Viewed in the context of the exquisitely contrasting, silk-green walls, and outlined in neat narrow bands, it assumes the appearance of an enormous abstract painting.

The solid colours and uninterrupted surfaces of the walls, floor and ceiling enhance the sense of spaciousness in what is, in fact, a comparatively small room. The deep plum ceiling has a lowered, intimate effect, focusing attention on the vase set just above floor level.

Plum, grey and beige, with a single note of sky-blue, combine to provide both peace and sophistication in this guest-house of an Osaka mansion. The award-winning design makes some concessions to the possibility of Western visitors – such as the sleekly curved, built-in wardrobe, related integrally to the expanded and abstracted *tokonoma*.

The lush, enveloping green of this urban room could be in deference to the fact that normally a wall would have slid back to reveal a delightful garden vista. A matching green continues across the floor in the fresh *tatami* mats.

The gloss surfaces of the platform and window recesses add an element of gentle sheen where they catch the light which is diffused through translucent windows – a contemporary interpretation of the old-fashioned rice-paper type.

The floor and wardrobe are toned to match the natural colour of the *tatami* mats used for sitting or lying. Their standard size, roughly 3 by 6 feet, is the unit of measure by which Japanese room sizes are traditionally expressed.

DUGGIE FIELDS

'I've treated this room as a painting,' says London artist Duggie Fields. 'I cannot understand how artists can do things on canvas and not apply the same things outside of it. I have painted my clothes, tried doing fabrics, murals, designing sofas and chairs, but as I try everything, I keep the canvas as my main thing all the time.'

To sum up his interior style simply as 'fifties' is misleading. In fact, it incorporates items from nearly every decade this century. The key is in his frame of reference as a painter – the influences of modern giants such as Mondrian, Pollock, Miró, Dali. Their work was gradually assimilated into the mass-market design of the fifties, and their motifs and techniques have been adapted, both directly and indirectly, by Duggie Fields as painter and as his own decorator.

'I like black, white, red, yellow and blue . . . minimal symbolism.' He credits the combined influences of Mondrian and children's comics with regard to his penchant for intense primaries and hard-edged lines. These also satisfy his taste for an active, stimulating atmosphere. 'If you don't do anything about manipulating your environment, it will manipulate you. Too often, it can deaden you.' He keeps boredom at bay with the surreal – random limbs, lips, torsos strewn through the house: a theme that has subsequently emerged in his work. He feeds on jokes. 'Humour is serious; anything that uplifts one is serious.' The upright brick on the table was left by burglars who used it to break in. He painted it.

Although he acknowledges that it is less than comfortable, he says, 'This is my treat room, because for me it does have this escape function – a room to enjoy.' It evolves continually. 'I repaint, redraw, redefine. I find the atmosphere needs revitalizing regularly.'

The blue of the ceiling was taken directly from the skies in the landscapes he was painting at the time he began decorating this room.

The wood-grain effect was inspired by one similar where he stayed in New York. 'I didn't have this side of the room worked out to begin with. I wondered if I could handle that sort of effect and thought I might as well try.' The same browns and beiges appear in the foreground of the mural on the wall between the windows.

The light switch has been meticulously decorated to match the door and table. 'If it is a matter of painting over a thing or making a feature of it, I feature it – electric sockets, ventilator grille, telephone.'

The frenetic, black and white gloss treatment of the table and door is a deliberate, attention-getting device. 'It was supposed to be *Angst* – the emotions showing through. I was thinking of painting as I was doing it. I wanted messiness in controlled areas.'

Stylized palettes – his signature motif – form the sides to this custom-built, black, Rietveld-style chair. The blobs of paint are, appropriately, the primaries he emphasizes in his work. The wood-grain effect matches the wall.

White walls are the backdrop he prefers for his paintings; all the walls in his studio/workroom are white.

The large painting entitled *All That Glitters* (*Portrait of Joan Quinn*) commemorates the pulsating night view from the hills overlooking Los Angeles and the 'quite magical' LA housewife in whose house he stayed. It embodies the principles of colour and line which he has synthesized from his permanent repertoire of influences – comic art to Mondrian.

This work, '*Those Who Love Their Own Creations Too Much Fall Into Bondage*', is, among other things, an example of how items around the house eventually find themselves immortalized as subject matter in his paintings. The heavy black chain he uses to hang his canvasses elsewhere in the room is here draped over the top as an integral part of the composition. Such chain appears painted into later works. The ever-present primaries occur as accents.

The shiny, red satin sofa is also custom-made in his favourite colour. Cushions, here disconcertingly arranged like gappy teeth, suit the stimulating, offbeat surroundings. 'Actually they do all meet when they are lying the right way, but I like changing it about – sticking the odd arm between cushions, and so on.'

Duggie dislikes curtains, so the glass doors and windows have been decorated with lengths of plastic tape. 'I twisted them very carefully to get rhythms of colour. There are two reds to one black, but the twists are alternate so it picks up the red. I experimented quite a lot before I did it.' The frames are painted in the same '*Angst*' style as the table and door.

He calls his orange trousers 'a conscious attempt to wear something one seldom sees. I have a balancing reaction – if I see a lot of something I tend to go the other way.' Furnishings like the wicker display-dummy legs, with wry 'fig-leaf', are characteristic of Duggie Fields's personal style.

The action-painted floor recalls not only Jackson Pollock's canvasses, but Duggie Fields's own spontaneous, youthful experiments when he did outdoor dribble painting, letting the colour drop from different heights to see how the wind would carry it. He wanted to use the technique somewhere in his home, but was a bit apprehensive about so large a commitment as the floor. 'I made a mistake in using gloss paint for the dribble effect as it took too long to dry and also wrinkled, drying on top but not underneath. It is tiled and was originally painted different colours, which helps give a nice base texture, and I quite like it where it shows through . . . I used several layers of polyurethane sealant but it could have done with more.'

BETSEY JOHNSON

Betsey Johnson thinks pink. Her Manhattan loft borrows colours from the clothes that she designs: exuberant and original, without a hint of snobbery. Her fashion sense frees her to decorate in a quick-change style. This look does not have to be forever; it is emphatically for *now*.

Betsey, first of all, needs space. She grew up not in the city but in rural Connecticut, where she studied art and dance. A studio atmosphere suits her, but such large interiors are expensive and hard to come by in the city, unless one can transform this type of industrial property.

The loft is 3,000 square feet in area and has a mass of pipes, wiring and support columns. Betsey's treatment of it is a humorous, feminine riposte to the conventional high-tech trick of featuring the functional; she has opted for universal camouflage. Acres of bubble-gum pink set the place aglow.

Dynamic contrasts are created using apple green and black. Green against pink is a variation on Betsey's favourite complementary pair, green and red. Black and pink in tandem represents for her the teaming of solidity and frivolity – and nostalgia for the rock-and-roll fifties.

Paint, the speediest medium, has put this bold and unusual scheme into gear with an energy that implies, 'If you can't stand it, I can change it in a minute. I can do *anything*.'

The all-over pink hides unfortunate architectural details, pulls the space together and even gives a rosy, candle-lit glow to the complexion of anyone who enters. One of Betsey's inspirations for choosing this shade was a holiday in Mexico just before moving into the loft. The Mexican skies were a dawn-to-dark spectacle of rose and magenta. In the same way, the pink she has used changes constantly with the changing light.

The brilliant apple green; seen through the circular opening in the pink wall, has the impact of a modern painting. This particular pink and green are complementary – direct opposites on the colour wheel – causing them to seem almost to vibrate next to one another, giving the room a buzz.

Shine bounces off the chrome of the furniture and the polished wood floor, as well as the many gloss – black accessory items, giving sparkle to the space

Slick black surfaces in different contexts – a plastic shower curtain, a vinyl two-seater, spray-painted venetian blinds and Art Deco lacquer furniture – show starkly against the pink. The gloss, though, reflects the pink to give the black a warm cast. Says Betsey, 'Pink for Mexico, black for New York.'

The glimpsed aquamarine WC is in a blue chromatically compatible with the pink and green – and just as outrageous. It makes a jazzy contrast with the surrounding pink.

The Art Deco influence is a perennial favourite with designers in general and New Yorkers in particular. The fireplace is purely decorative, just propped against the wall for effect.

Betsey Johnson and daughter Lulu enjoy a home that offers the same freedom of movement as a dance studio, in colours that make you want to kick up your heels. Spontaneity and nostalgia meet in a scheme that evokes the thirties, the fifties and this minute.

161

GLOSSARY

A

Achromatic colours The 'colourless colours' – white, black, greys and silvery metallics – devoid of hue.

Advancing colours The *warm*, long-wavelength colours of the *spectrum* – reds, oranges and yellows – which seem to bring surfaces closer to the eye.

Analogous colours Closely related colours, neighbours on the *colour wheel* – yellow, yellow-green, green and blue-green, for example.

Antiquing Artificial ageing of wood and painted finishes by various processes. Glazes with coloured washes tone down bright surfaces, which may then be 'distressed' with paint stripper and abrasion, or bored with simulated worm holes, to make them look time-worn.

B

Brightness An ambiguous term, technically meaning highly saturated when describing a colour, but also used as a synonym for lightness.

C

Celadon Delicate shades of green ranging from grey to blue, named after the classic Chinese porcelain glazed in these colours.

Chroma The measurement of a colour's intensity or *saturation*. A pure colour is high in chroma; a greyed or dull one is low.

Collage In decorating, a composition of materials and objects pasted over a surface. Often unifying lines, subject matter or colour themes impose a discreet order on their naturally random character.

Colour The attribute of a visual sensation, or by extension an object or light, that can be named by such terms as red, yellow, blue and so on. Perceived colour has three basic dimensions: *hue, saturation* and *lightness*.

Colour solid An imaginary systematic arrangement of colours in three dimensions: *hue* runs around the neutral axis (which is analogous to the *colour wheel*) keeping the spectral order, beginning and ending with red. Saturation extends radially and horizontally from the central neutral axis, so that pure colours are outermost and greyed colours innermost; *lightness* extends top to bottom, relating to an *achromatic* central axis with white as the 'north pole', through deepening greys, to black as the 'south pole'.

Colour wheel A convenient circular depiction of the relationship between *primary, secondary* and *tertiary* colours, arranged clockwise in their spectral order, beginning and ending with red. *Analogous colours* border one another; *complementary colours* are precisely opposite each other, making the wheel a useful reference for colour schemes.

Combing A decorative finish whereby a wavy or grained effect is produced by running a toothed strip of plastic, rubber or card through a still-wet, deeply tinted top glaze to reveal the dry, lighter base coat beneath.

Complementary colours Pairs of colours which, when mixed together, produce grey: red and green, blue and orange, yellow and purple, for instance. They sit directly opposite one another on the *colour wheel*, and, in use, are dynamically contrasting.

Cool colours Generally those in the shorter-wavelength, green-to-blue-to-violet half of the *spectrum*, although yellowy greens and reddish violets are considered 'intermediate' in temperature. The *colours* with blue and green content have naturally cool associations with sky, water and foliage.

D

Dye Soluble colouring matter. When a dye is applied to a material from solution, it penetrates and combines with the underlying fabric. It always reduces the *lightness* of the fabric so can never dye to a paler shade.

G

Glaze A transparent top coat of paint, commonly oil-based, used to modify or seal a base coat.

Graining An artful simulation of natural wood grain using paint; often exaggerated, and not necessarily in true wood tones.

Grey An *achromatic* colour, intermediate in lightness between white and black and decoratively *neutral*, although it can appear coloured under coloured light.

H

Hue The 'colour of colour'; the attribute of colour by which it is distinguished from another. All colours are judged to be similar to one, or a proportion of two, of the *spectral* hues: red, orange, yellow, green, blue and violet. Scarlet and pink, although different colours, are related by hue. Physically, hue is determined by wavelength.

I

Intensity A synonym for *saturation*.

L

Light Electromagnetic radiation capable of stimulating the *eye* to produce visual sensations. All colour is composed of light.

Lightness The dimension of a *surface colour* falling between white and black, through an intermediate series of greys. Also sometimes referred to as *value* – the amount of incident light a colour sample appears to reflect. The measure of how white or black, light or dark a colour appears.

M

Marbling A decorative finish imitative of marble, achieved with paint; it may be literal or stylized. It flourished in eighteenth-century France and Italy and remains a popular means of producing grand effects at nominal cost.

Metamerism The optical effect that causes two colour surfaces which look identical under one type of light to look different under another. For example, tiles and carpet or fabric that match under a shop's fluorescent light may vary in daylight. Two such surfaces are called a metameric pair. Conversely, a metameric match is achieved by colouring two materials with different dyes or pigments to look identical under specific lighting conditions.

Monochromatic Although literally it means containing only one colour, in decorating terms it describes a scheme based around a single colour family; so it might consist of sky-blue, Wedgewood blue and navy. The scheme could incorporate various *achromatics* – white, grey, silver – and still be termed monochromatic.

N

Neutral In decorating, a colour which does not clash or conflict with any other, and, therefore, may be incorporated into any scheme. In addition to the *achromatics*, beiges, browns, fawns, and so on, which take their colour from natural sources such as wood, sand or stone are regarded as neutrals, as are the materials themselves.

P

Pastels In decorating, the soft, white-added *tints* of a colour. When expressed as pastels, normally contrasting colours are reconciled.

Patina The soft lustre produced on an antique surface by age and wear.

Pigment An insoluble colouring material which has to be applied to a surface in conjunction with a binding material. Pigments coat the colour of the underlying surface rather than combining with it.

Primary colours Red, blue and yellow. The three pure, unmixed colours from which all others are derived, and which cannot themselves be produced by any mixture. Green is considered a 'psychological' primary, even though it can be produced by mixing yellow and blue.

Prismatic colours The *spectral colours* which appear when a beam of sunlight is diffracted through a prism (a transparent glass or plastic block of triangular cross-section).

Purity (of colour) A synonym for *saturation*.

R

Receding colours The *cool* shorter-wavelength colours, such as blue, green and violet, which appear to move away, giving an impression of distance and space.

Retina The light-sensitive inner surface of the *eye* on which images are projected by the lens.

Reveal The internal, side surface of a window or door, frequently flaring outward at an angle inside the room to enhance natural light.

S

Saturation The term used to describe the strength or vividness of a *hue*. Red, for example, can range in saturation from a greyish dove-pink to a rich vermilion. High saturation indicates a pure colour; low saturation a greyed one.

Secondary colours Orange, green and purple – the colours resulting from an equal mixture of two *primaries*.

Shade In common usage, a colour differing slightly from a specified *hue* or colour (for example, 'a shade of blue' or 'a greyish-green shade').

Technically, a term used to define degrees of *lightness*, indicating a pure colour that has been mixed with grey or black.

Spatter A decorative finish in which colours are spattered or splashed over a solid-colour ground.

Spectral colours The rainbow colours of the *spectrum*, seen when sunlight is diffracted through a prism: red, orange, yellow, green, blue and violet. They are perfectly saturated and over most of the spectrum are vivid; they do not contain pinks, purples, browns or greys.

Spectrum The coloured image formed when white light is spread out, according to its wavelength, by being passed through a prism. The relative intensities of the colours in the spectrum of, say, artificial light will differ from those in the spectrum of sunlight.

Split complementary A three-colour scheme using one half of a *complementary* pair and the two colours lying either side of the other half on the *colour wheel*, such as blue with yellow-orange and red-orange.

Sponging A decorative finish in which a top colour is applied over a solid base coat using a natural *sea sponge* or porous artificial sponge, giving a random, lightly flecked appearance. Normally an additive procedure, but it may also be practised using the sponge partially to remove a still-wet top glaze.

Staining A method of colouring wood, first practised in seventeenth-century England. Originally used for furniture, but now extended to floors, using either natural or artificial colours.

Stencilling A decorative technique whereby a surface is covered with a mask with the stencil design cut out so that when paint, dye or stain is applied through the openings, the desired pattern will appear on the surface below.

Stippling A decorative technique giving a soft, textured finish. The top colour is applied over the dry base coat, using the tip of a stiff-bristled stippling brush; or the brush may be used simply to pound the wet surface.

Surface colour Colour belonging to (or perceived as belonging to) a surface that sends (or appears to send) light to the eye by diffuse reflection. The perception of surface colours is strongly influenced by their context and by the nature of their illumination.

T

Tertiary colour Colours lying between a *primary* and a *secondary* on the *colour wheel*. Or, intermediate colours resulting from a mixture of two *secondary colours*, the tones varying with the proportion of the mixture, such as russet and olive.

Tint A colour or *pigment* containing a large amount of white, referred to in decorating as a *pastel*. In common usage, a colour appearing weakly to modify another ('beige with a pink tint').

Tone A synonym for *lightness*. Also, a colour differing slightly in any way from a specified colour ('a tone of green'). A colour that appreciably modifies another ('green with a bluish tone').

Tonal value The gradations of one colour from light to dark. Pink is a light *value* (or *tint*) of red; maroon is a dark value (or *shade*).

Triadic colour scheme A scheme based on three colours or colour families equidistant on the *colour wheel*, such as the three *primaries* or three *secondaries*, in either bold or muted tones – a bright red, yellow and blue, or discreet mauve, pumpkin yellow and moss green, for instance.

'Trompe-l'œil' From the French, to 'fool the eye' – decorative illusions, typically of a third dimension, or imitative of costly materials (marble, fine wood) or elaborate architectural detail.

V

Value A synonym for *lightness*.

W

Warm colours Those in the long-wavelength, red-orange-yellow half of the *colour wheel*. Also known as *advancing colours*. They can make walls appear to close in or make a small object look more important.

Wash A thin mixture of one colour applied over another; similar to a glaze.

White light A mixture of all visible wavelengths of light in the same proportions in which they are found in sunlight.

GAZETTEER

In the places listed below, the reader may find colour used in interiors in interesting and stimulating ways.

We cannot pretend that this list is in any way definitive, but we do hope that it is sufficiently comprehensive to serve as a guide to those wishing to use overseas trips, or even domestic travel, as an opportunity for finding inspiration.

Additionally, although not listed here, the museums – both great and small – in our towns and cities contain some of the most magnificent riches of our colour heritage. Visits to these are recommended, as is a tour of any local furniture and fabric manufacturers' shops or showrooms.

If pressed for time while travelling, a handful of postcards of noteworthy buildings can often furnish you with a wealth of colour ideas.

AUSTRALIA
NEW SOUTH WALES
Bedervale, Braidwood
Brownlon Hill, Cobbity
Camden Park, Menangle
Havilah, Mudgee
Kelvin, Bringelly
SOUTH AUSTRALIA
Martindale Hall, Mintara
Yallum Park, Penola
TASMANIA
Clarendon, Evandale
Woolmers, Longford
VICTORIA
Merrang, Hexam
Murndal, Hamilton
Werribee Park, Werribee

AUSTRIA
VIENNA
Hofburg
Majolica House
Schönbrunn Palace
The Upper and Lower Belvedere
The Winter Palace

BELGIUM
BRUSSELS
Hôtel van Eetvelde
Victor Horta's house

CHINA
PEKING
Dragon Wall, Forbidden City
T'ai-ho-Men (Palace of Great Peace) Forbidden City
Tian Tan (Temple of Heaven)

DENMARK
COPENHAGEN AND ENVIRONS
Amalienborg Palace, Amalienborg Square
Rosenborg
Kronborg Castle, nr Elsinore
Frederiksborg Castle Hillerød

EAST GERMANY
DRESDEN
Zwinger Palace
POTSDAM
Sans Souci

EGYPT
CAIRO
Cairo Museum

ENGLAND
AVON
Claverton Manor, (The American Museum), Bath
1 Royal Crescent, Bath
BEDFORDSHIRE
Luton Hoo, Luton
BUCKINGHAMSHIRE
Waddesdon Manor, nr Aylesbury
CHESHIRE
Adlington Hall, nr Macclesfield
Bramall Hall, Bramhall, Stockport
CUMBRIA
Levens Hall, nr Kendal
DERBYSHIRE
Chatsworth, Bakewell
Haddon Hall, nr Bakewell
Hardwick Hall, nr Chesterfield
Kedleston Hall, nr Derby
DEVONSHIRE
Arlington Court, nr Barnstable
Castle Drogo, nr Chagford
Knightshayes Court, nr Tiverton
CO. DURHAM
The Bowes Museum, Barnard Castle
GLOUCESTERSHIRE
Sudeley Castle, Winchcombe, nr Cheltenham
GREATER MANCHESTER
Heaton Hall, Heaton Park, Prestwich
HAMPSHIRE
Beaulieu Abbey, Beaulieu, nr Lymington
Jane Austen's house, Chawton nr Alton
Stratfield Saye House, Reading
HERTFORDSHIRE
Hatfield House, Hatfield
KENT
Knole, Sevenoaks

Leeds Castle, nr Maidstone
Pattyndenne Manor, Goudhurst
Penshurst Place, Tunbridge Wells
LEICESTERSHIRE
Quenby Hall, Hungarton
LONDON
Apsley House, The Wellington Museum, Hyde Park Corner
Chiswick House, Chiswick
Fenton House, Hampstead
Hampton Court Palace, Hampton Court, East Molesey
Keats House, Hampstead
Kenwood House, Hampstead
Kew Palace, (Dutch House), Kew
William Morris Gallery, Lloyd Park
Orleans House, Riverside, Twickenham
Osterley Park House, Osterley
Syon House, Brentford, Middlesex
Victoria and Albert Museum, South Kensington
NORTH YORKSHIRE
Castle Howard, nr York
OXFORDSHIRE
Blenheim Palace, Woodstock
Buscott Park, nr Farringdon
SHROPSHIRE
Attingham Park, nr Shrewsbury
SOMERSET
Monacute House, nr Yeovil
WARWICKSHIRE
Ragley Hall, Alcester, nr Stratford-on-Avon
WARWICKSHIRE
Warwick Castle, Warwick
WEST SUSSEX
Arundel Castle, Arundel
Parham, Pulborough
Petworth House, Petworth
The Royal Pavilion, Brighton
WEST YORKSHIRE
Harewood House, Leeds
WILTSHIRE
Longleat House, Warminster

FRANCE
HAUTE SAÔNE
Notre Dame de Haut, Ronchamp
LOIRE VALLEY
Azay-le-Rideau, Indre-et-Loire
Château de Chambord, Loir-et-Cher
Château de Cheverny, Loir-et-Cher
NORMANDY
Château de Balleroy Calvados, nr Bayeux
Monet's house, Giverny, nr Vernon, Eure
PARIS AND ENVIRONS
Chantilly, Oise

Château de la Malmaison, Rueil-Malmaison
Maxims, 3 Rue Royale
Musée de Cluny, 23 Boulevard St Michel
Musée des Gobelins, 42 Avenue des Gobelins
Château de Fontainebleau, Seine-et-Marne
Château de Maisons-Lafitte, Yvelines
Château de Vaux-le-Vicomte, Maincy, Seine-et-Marne
Chateau de Versailles, Seine-et-Oise
St Germain-en-Laye, Yvelines
Villa Savoie, Poissy
PROVENCE
Chapelle de Vence, Vence, nr Nice
Matisse's house, nr Nice

GREECE
CORFU
The Palace of St Michael and St George, Corfu town
CRETE
Herakleion Museum, Herakleion

HOLLAND
THE HAGUE
Huis Ten Bosch

INDIA
DELHI
Jama Masjid, Old Delhi
Presidential Palace, New Delhi
The Red Fort, Old Delhi
GUJARAT
Jami Jasjid, Ahmadabad
Maison Shodan, Ahmadabad
Makarpura Palace, nr Baroda
Mill Owners' Association Building, Ahmadabad
Wankaner Palace, Wankaner
MADHYA PRADESH
Painted Palace, Gwalior
PUNJAB
The Capitol and the High Court, Chandigarh
Golden Temple, Amritsar
RAJASTHAN
Lake Palace Hotel, Udaipur
The Palace of Man Singh I, Amber
UTTAR PRADESH
Taj Mahal, Agra
Tomb of Akbar, Agra

IRAN
ISFAHAN
The Great Mosque

ITALY
NAPLES
The Royal Palace, Piazza Plebiscito
The Royal Palace, Caserta, nr Naples
NOVARA
Palazzo Borromeo, Isola Bella, Lake
    Maggiore
PIEDMONT
Castello Reale de Raconigi, nr Turin
Palazzo Madama, Piazzo Castello,
    Turin
ROME
Palazzo Doria
The Quirinal Palace. Piazza del
    Quiranal
SICILY
Villa ai Colli, Mt Pellegrino, nr
    Palermo
TUSCANY
Castello de Sammezzano
Davanzati Palace, Florence
Uffizi Art Gallery, Piazza degli Uffizi,
    Florence
VENICE
Museo Fortuny, Palazzo Fortuny,
    Campo S Benedetto
Palazzo Ducale (Doge's Palace)

JAPAN
KYŌTO
Katsura Palace
Heian Jingu
The Kinkaku (Golden Pavilion)
Kitayama Palace
Kyōto Gosho (Imperial Palace)
Nijo Castle
Shugakuin Villa

NORTHERN IRELAND
Ardress House, nr Portadown, Co.
    Armagh
Castle Coole, Enniskillen, Co.
    Fermanagh
Castle Ward, Strang Ford, Co. Down
Mount Stewart House, Grey Abbey,
    Co. Down
Springhill, Moneymore, Co.
    Londonderry

PORTUGAL
LISBON AND ENVIRONS
Paço de Vila, Sintra
Palácio da Fronteira, Fronteira
Palácio da Pena, Sintra
Palácio da Queluz, Queluz
Seteais, Sintra

SCOTLAND
ARGYLLSHIRE
Inverarary Castle, Inverarary

GLASGOW
Glasgow School of Art
Hill House
PEEBLESSHIRE
Traquair, Innerleithen

SPAIN
ANDALUSIA
The Alhambra, Granada
BARCELONA
Casa Batló, Paseo de Gracia
Casa Milá, Paseo de Gracia
Palacio Güell, Conde del Asalto
CORDOBA
The Great Mosque
MADRID AND ENVIRONS
El Escorial
The Royal Palace in Madrid
The Royal Palace of Aranjuez

SYRIA
DAMASCUS
The Great Mosque

SWEDEN
STOCKHOLM AND ENVIRONS
Haga Slot, (including the Haga
    Pavilion in the grounds)
The Royal Palace of Drottningholm,
    (including the China Palace in the
    grounds)
The Royal Palace
Tullgarn

THAILAND
BANGKOK
The Grand Palace
Wat Arun (Temple of the Dawn)
Wat Saket

USA
ALABAMA
The Bellingrath Home, Theodore
ARIZONA
Taliesin West, Phoenix
CALIFORNIA
J. Paul Getty Museum, 17985 Pacific
    Coast Highway, Malibu
San Simeon (Hearst Castle)
Scotty's Castle, Grapevine Canyon
CONNECTICUT
Mark Twain House, 351 Farmington
    Avenue, Hartford
DELAWARE
Amstel House, New Castle
Old Dutch House, New Castle
The Winterthur Museum, Wilmington
FLORIDA
Ca' d' Zan, The John Ringling
    Residence, Sarasota

Hemingway House and Museum, 907
    Whitehead, Key West
Henry Morrison Flagler Museum, 71
    Whitehall Way, Palm Beach
Vizcaya, South Bayshore Drive, Miami
GEORGIA
Swan House, Atlanta
LOUISIANA
San Francisco Plantation House,
    between New Orleans and Baton
    Rouge
Shadows-on-the-Teche, 117E Main
    Street, New Iberia
MARYLAND
Hollyhill, Friendship
MASSACHUSETTS
Capen House, Topsfield
Whipple House, Ipswich
MISSISSIPPI
Longwood, Natchez
NEW YORK
The Henry Clay Frick Museum, Fifth
    Avenue
Metropolitan Museum of Art, Fifth
    Avenue
Milligan House, Saratoga Springs,
    (reconstructed in Brooklyn Mus.)
Van Cortland House, Van Cortland
    Park
NORTH CAROLINA
Biltmore Mansion, nr Asheville
PENNSYLVANIA
Andalusia, Biddle Estate, nr
    Philadelphia
Clivedon, 6401 Germantown Avenue,
    Philadelphia
Falling Water, Bear Run
Strawberry Mansion, Philadelphia
RHODE ISLAND
Belcourt Castle, Newport
The Breakers, Newport
SOUTH CAROLINA
Seabrooke House, nr Charleston
VIRGINIA
Carter's Grove, nr Williamsburg
The Governor's Palace, Williamsburg
Kenmore, Fredericksburg
Monticello, Charlottesville
Williamsburg Restorations,
    Williamsburg
WASHINGTON DC
The Peacock Room,
    Freer Gallery of Art
WISCONSIN
Taliesin, Spring Green

USSR
LENINGRAD AND ENVIRONS
Tsarskoe Selo, Pushkin
The Winter Palace

WALES
SOUTH GLAMORGAN
Cardiff Castle, Cardiff
Castell Coch, Tongwynlais, nr Cardiff
GWYNEDD
Portmeirion, Penrhyndeudraeth
ISLE OF ANGLESEY
Plas Newydd
POWYS
Powis Castle, Welshpool
Trelydan Hall, Welshpool

WEST GERMANY
BAVARIA
Palace of the Princes of Thurn and
    Taxis, Regensburg
Pommersfelden Castle, Bamberg
The Residenz, Münich
Schloss Herenchiemsee,
    Lake Chiemsee, nr Münich
Schloss Linderhof, nr Oberammergau
Schloss Neuschwanstein, nr Füssen
Schloss Nymphenburg, (including the
    pavilions: the Amalienburg, the
    Badenburg, the Pagodenburg) nr
    Münich
Schloss Schleissheim, nr Münich
FRANCONIA
The Residenz, Würzburg
Schloss Eremitage, nr Bayreuth

BIBLIOGRAPHY

The following is a list of books which have been consulted during the preparation of *Living With Colour* or are recommended by the author as a source of colour inspiration:

Aragon, Louis (Translated by Stewart, Jean) *Henri Matisse* William Collins & Sons, London, 1972

Architectural Digest *American Interiors* Viking Press Inc, New York, 1978

Arthaud, Claude *Dream Palaces* Thames & Hudson Ltd, London, 1973

Bakst, Léon (Translated from the French by Melville, Harry) *The Decorative Art of Léon Bakst* Constable & Co, London, 1972; Dover Publications Inc, New York, 1972

Baldwin, Billy *Billy Baldwin Decorates* Holt, Rinehart & Winston, New York, 1972

Bamford Smith, Clive *Builders in the Sun: Five Mexican Architects* Architectural Book Pub Co, New York, 1967

Battersby, Martin *The Decorative Twenties* Studio Vista Ltd, London, 1969; Walker Publishing Co, New York, 1969

Battersby, Martin *The Decorative Thirties* Studio Vista Ltd, London, 1969; Walker Publishing Co, New York, 1971

Bentman, Reinhard and Lickes, Heinrich *Palaces of Europe* Cassell Ltd, London, 1978

Bishop, Adele and Lord, Cile *The Art of Decorative Stencilling* Thames & Hudson Ltd, London, 1976; Viking Press Inc, New York, 1976

Boesiger, Willy *Le Corbusier Last Works* Praeger Publishers Inc, New York, 1970

Bossert, Helmuth *An Encyclopaedia of Colour Decoration from the Earliest Times to the Middle of the XIXth Century* Ernst Wasmuth Ltd, Berlin, 1928

Brown, Erica *Interior Views (Design at its Best)* Thames & Hudson Ltd, London, 1980; Viking Press Inc, New York, 1980

Carrington, Noel *Design and Decoration in the Home* Country Life Ltd, London, 1938

Čelebonović, Aleksa *The Heyday of Salon Painting* Thames & Hudson Ltd, London, 1974; Harry N. Abrams Inc, New York, 1974

Clark. Kenneth *Civilisation* British Broadcasting Corporation & John Murray, London, 1969; Harper & Row Publishers Inc, New York, 1972

Clifford, Derek *Art and Understanding* Evelyn, Adams & Mackay Ltd, London, 1968; New York Graphic Society, Greenwich, Connecticut, 1968

Conran, Terence *The Bed and Bath Book* Mitchell Beazley Ltd, London, 1978; Crown Publishers Inc, New York, 1978

Conran, Terence *The House Book* Mitchell Beazley Ltd, London, 1974; Crown Publishers Inc, New York, 1974

Conran, Terence *The Kitchen Book* Mitchell Beazley Ltd, London, 1977; Crown Publishers Inc, New York, 1977

Demachy, Alain *Interior Architecture and Decoration* Studio Vista Ltd, London, 1974; William Morrow & Co, New York, 1974

De Osma, Guillermo *Mariano Fortuny: His Life and Work* Aurum Press, London, 1980; Rizzoli International Publications Inc, Secaucus, New Jersey, 1980

Di San Lazzaro, G. (Ed.) *Homage to Wassily Kandinsky* Edeling Publishing, London, 1976; Leon Amael Publisher, New York, 1975

Duveen, Edward J. *Colour in the Home* George Allen & Co Ltd, London, 1911

Feder, Norman *American Indian Art* Harry N. Abrams Inc, New York, 1970

Feldman, Edmund Burke *Varieties of Visual Experience* Harry N. Abrams Inc, New York, 1973

Fermigier, André *Pierre Bonnard* Thames & Hudson Ltd, London, 1970; Harry N. Abrams Inc, New York, 1969

Gombrich, E.H. *The Story of Art* Phaidon Press Ltd, Oxford, 1972; E.P. Dutton & Co, New York, 1972

Grant, Ian (Ed) *Great Interiors* Hamlyn Publishing Group Ltd, London, 1967; Spring Books, New York, 1967

Guild, Robin *The Finishing Touch* Mitchell Beazley Ltd, London, 1979; (Homeworks) Van Nostrand Reinhold Co, New York, 1979

Guild, Tricia *Soft Furnishings* Pan Books Ltd, London and Sydney, 1980; Farrar, Straus & Giroux Inc, New York, 1980

Hansen, H.J. (Ed) *European Folk Art* Thames & Hudson Ltd, London 1968

Hayward, Helena (Ed) *World Furniture* Paul Hamlyn London, 1965; McGraw Hill Book Co, New York, 1965

Innes, Jocasta *Paint Magic* Windward/Berger Paints, London, 1981; Van Nostrand Reinhold Co, New York, 1981

Janson, H.W. *A History of Art* Thames & Hudson Ltd, London, 1978; Harry N. Abrams Inc, New York

Johnson, P. *The National Trust Book of British Castles* Weidenfeld & Nicolson Ltd, London, 1978; G.P. Putnam & Sons, New York, 1978

Jones, Owen *The Grammar of Ornament* Bernard Quaritch, London, 1910

Joyes, Claire *Monet at Giverny* Mathew Miller Dunbar Ltd, London, 1975; The Two Containers Publishing Group Ltd, New York, 1977

Jullian, Rene *Fernand Léger* Editions Beyeler, Basle, 1970

Knon, Joan and Slesin, Suzanne *High Tech* Allen Lane Press, London, 1979; Clarkson N. Potter Inc, New York, 1979

Le Corbusier *The Radiant City* Faber & Faber Ltd, London, 1964; Orion Press, New York, 1967

Lipman, J. and Winchester, A. *The Flowering of American Folk Art 1776-1876* Thames & Hudson Ltd, London, 1974; Viking Press Inc, New York, 1974

Lüscher, Dr Max (Translated and edited by Scott, Ian A.) *The Lüscher Colour Test* Pan Books Ltd, London, 1971; Random House, New York

Mekhitarian, Arpag *Egyptian Painting* Skira/Macmillan London Ltd, 1978

Moody, Ella (Ed) *Decorative Art in Modern Furnishings* Studio Vista Ltd, London, 1972; Viking Press Inc, New York, 1972

Myers, Bernard L. and Copplestone Trewin *The Macmillan Encyclopaedia of Art* Macmillan London Ltd, 1977; Holt, Rinehart & Winston, New York, 1970

Nicholson, N. *Great Houses of the Western World* Hamlyn Publishing Group Ltd, London, 1972

O'Neill, Isobel *The Art of Painted Finish for Furniture and Decoration* William Morrow & Co, New York, 1971

Oliver, Paul (Ed) *Shelter in Africa* Barrie & Jenkins, London, 1971; Frederick A. Praeger Inc, New York, 1971

Parker, Derek and Julia *The Compleat Astrologer* Mitchell Beazley Ltd, London, 1971; McGraw Hill Book Co, New York, 1971

Patmore, Derek *Colour Schemes and Modern Furnishings* 'The Studio', London and New York, Reprinted 1947

Pavey, Donald (Ed) *Colour* Mitchell Beazley Ltd, London, 1980; Viking Press Inc, New York, 1980

Rowell, Margit *Miró* Harry N. Abrams Inc, New York, 1970

Selz, Peter *Sam Francis* Harry N. Abrams Inc, New York, 1975

Shone, Richard *Bloomsbury Portraits: Vanessa Bell, Duncan Grant and their Circle* Phaidon Press Ltd, Oxford, 1976; E.P. Dutton & Co, New York, 1976

Sitwell, Sacheverell *Great Palaces* Weidenfeld & Nicolson Ltd, London, 1964; G.P. Putnam & Sons, New York, 1964

Skurka, Norma and Gili, Oberto *Underground Interiors* Quadrangle Books, New York, 1972

Stangos, Nikos (Ed) *David Hockney by David Hockney* Thames & Hudson Ltd, London, 1976; Harry N. Abrams Inc, New York, 1976

Street-Porter, Tim *Interiors* Omnibus Press, London, 1982; Quick Fox, New York, 1982

Tracy, Berry B. *19th Century America Furniture and Decorative Arts* Metropolitan Museum of Art, New York Graphic Society Ltd

Wichmann, Siegfried *Japonisme* Thames & Hudson Ltd, London, 1981; Harmony Books Inc, New York, 1981

Wilson, José and Leaman, Arthur *Decoration USA* Collier Macmillan Ltd, London, 1965; Macmillan Co, New York, 1965

Wilson, José and Leaman, Arthur *Colour in Decoration* Studio Vista Ltd, London, 1971; Van Nostrand Reinhold Ltd, New York, 1971

ACKNOWLEDGEMENTS

The Publishers wish to thank the designers, photographers and agencies listed below for their help in providing material for this book. The following abbreviations have been used:
t top; *b* bottom; *c* centre; *l* left; *r* right

Cover: Susan Zises Green, New York/Michael Dunne; Back cover: Clive Corless; 1 Elyse Lewin/Transworld Features; 3 Alain Dovifat/Brigitte Baert; 4/5 Norman McGrath; 6 Brigitte Baert; 8 Bonnard *Le Déjeuner* (c) A.D.A.G.P. Paris, 1982, Giraudon; 10/11 Bulloz; 12*l* William McQuitty; 13*l* Angelo Hornak; 13*tr* *Elle*/Transworld Features: 13*br Décoration:* Jacques Grange/Photo: Pascal Hinous/Agence Top; 14*l* Michael Holford/Courtesy of the Trustees of the British Museum; 14*r* John Bethell/National Trust; 15*tr* Mastro Raphaël/Robert Emmett Bright; 15*br* Mastro Raphaël/Robert Emmett Bright; 16*t* Scala; 16*b* Michael Holford/Victoria & Albert Museum; 17*tl* Giraudon/Musée des Gobelins, Paris; 17*bl* Victoria & Albert Museum; 17*tr* Scala; 17*br* Brighton Polytechnic; 18*t* Claus Hansmann; 18*cl* Sotheby's Chinese Department; 18*cr* Bavaria-Verlag; 18*b* David Mehta/Colorific!; 19*l* British Tourist Authority; 19*tr* The Bridgeman Art Library; 19*br* Sanderson & Sons Ltd; 20 William McQuitty; 20/21 Ursel Borstell/Camera Press; 21*tl* Royal Borough of Kensington & Chelsea; 21*tr* Bruno de Hamel; 21*b* Academy Editions; 22/3 Michael Holford/The American Museum in Britain; 24*t* P. Berenger/Rapho; 24*b* H.R. Uthoff/The Image Bank; 24/5 Ianthe Ruthven/Michael Holford Library; 25 Clive Corless; 26 Aspect Picture Library; 27*t* Robert Harding Associates; 27*b* Alan Hutchison Library; 28*t* Clive Corless; 28*b* C. Sarramon/Rapho; 29 Victoria & Albert Museum; 30 Ernst Haas/John Hillelson Agency; 30/31 Denver Art Museum, catalogue no: 1928.97; 31 Angelo Hornak/Museum of Mankind; 32 John Moss/Colorific!; 32/3 Paul Fusco/John Hillelson Agency; 34*t* Orion Press; 34*b* J. Alex Langley/Aspect Picture Library; 35 Orion Press; 36/7 Michael Nicholson/Elizabeth Whiting & Associates; 42/51 Clive Corless; 52/3 L.M. Kingcome Ltd; 54 Clive Corless; 55*l* Derry Moore; 55*r* Clive Corless; 56 Clive Corless; 56/7 Derry Moore; 57 Clive Corless; 58/9 *Zuhause*/Camera Press; 60/61 Bent Rej/Camera Press; 60/61 Clive Corless; 62/3 Paul Brierley; 64 Derry Moore; 64/5 Michael Boys/Susan Griggs Agency; 65 Robert Emmett Bright; 66 *Schöner Wohnen*/Camera Press; 67*t* Scoop/Transworld Features; 67*b* Elyse Lewin/Transworld Features; 68 Bill McLaughlin; 68/9 *Schöner Wohnen*/Camera Press; 70/71 *Schöner Wohnen*/Camera Press; 71 Apartment: Sofi Klarwein/Photo: J.P. Charbonnier/Agence Top: 74 Scoop/Transworld Features; 75 Robert Emmett Bright; 76 Jessica Strang; 76/7 Derry Moore; 77 Derry Moore; 78 Elyse Lewin/Transworld Features; 78/9 Bill McLaughlin; 79 Bruce Wolf; 80 Robert Emmett Bright; 80/81 Norman Eales; 81 Alain Dovifat/Brigitte Baert; 82/3 Clive

Corless; 84*t* *Schöner Wohnen*/Camera Press; 84*b* Tim Street-Porter/Elizabeth Whiting & Associates; 85 Michael Dunne; 86*t* *Schöner Wohnen*/Camera Press; 86*r* *Zuhause*/Camera Press; 86/7 *Schöner Wohnen*/Camera Press; 88 Bruno de Hamel; 88/9 Michael Dunne; 90/91 Clive Corless; 92/3 Clive Corless; 94 Clive Corless; 95 *Schöner Wohnen*/Camera Press; 96*l* Bruno de Hamel; 96*r* Scoop/Transworld Features; 97*l* *Schöner Wohnen*/Camera Press; 97*tr* Clive Corless; 97*cr* Clive Corless; 97*br* Clive Corless; 98*t* Michael Dunne; 98*b* Robert Emmett Bright; 99 Ezra Stoller/Esto; 100 *Schöner Wohnen*/Camera Press; 101*l* Morton Beebe/The Image Bank; 101*r* *Schöner Wohnen*/Camera Press; 102*l* Robert Emmett Bright; 102*r* Scoop/Transworld Features: 103 Michael Dunne; 104*t* Frank Spooner Pictures; 104*b* Dorma; 105 Marianne Haas/Brigitte Baert; 106*t* Michael Dunne; 106*b* National Magazine Co Ltd; 107*t* *Décoration:* Alain Demachy/Photo: Pascal Hinous/Agence Top; 107*b* Michael Dunne; 108*l* Laura Salvati/*Abitare*; 108*r* *Schöner Wohnen*/Camera Press; 109 Peter Aaron/Esto; 110*l* *Femina*/Camera Press; 110*r* *Schöner Wohnen*/Camera Press: 111 Michael Dunne; 112 Dorma; 112/3 Dorma; 113 Clive Corless; 114 *Schöner Wohnen*/Camera Press; 115 Norman McGrath; 116/7 Robert Emmett Bright; 118/9 Scoop/Transworld Features; 120/121 Masera/Camera Press; 122*t* Michael Nicholson/Elizabeth Whiting & Associates; 122*b* Samples: Roger Reynolds/Photos: Clive Corless; 123*tlr* Clive Corless; 123*b* Samples: Roger Reynolds/Photos: Clive Corless; 124*t* Clive Corless; 124*b* Samples: Roger Reynolds/Photos: Clive Corless; 125 Clive Corless; 126*l* Sample: Roger Reynolds/Photo: Clive Corless; 126*r* Michael Dunne; 127*l* *20ANS*/Transworld Features; 127*r* Samples: Roger Reynolds/Photos: Clive Corless; 128/9 *Schöner Wohnen*/Camera Press; 129 Samples: Roger Reynolds/Photos: Clive Corless; 130 Samples: Roger Reynolds/Photos: Clive Corless: 131*l* Scoop/Transworld Features; 131*r* Sample: Roger Reynolds/Photo: Clive Corless; 132*t* Marcus Harrison; 132*b* David Crips/Elizabeth Whiting & Associates; 133 Michael Boys/Susan Griggs Agency; 134*t* Jessica Strang; 134*b* Marcus Harrison; 135*l* Michael Boys/Susan Griggs Agency; 135*r* Clive Corless; 136/7 Derry Moore/Condé Nast Australia; 138 Lucinda Lambton/Vision International; 138/9 Marcus Harrison; 139 Lucinda Lambton/Vision International; 140/141 Alain Dovifat/Brigitte Baert; 142/3 *Elle*/Transworld Features; 144/5 Robert Emmett Bright; 146 Neil Lorimer/Elizabeth Whiting & Associates; 146/7 Tim Street-Porter/Elizabeth Whiting & Associates; 147 CVP Designs; 148/9 John Donat; 150/151 Lord Snowdon; 151*t* Lord Snowdon; 151*b* Derry Moore; 152/3 Pierre Boulat/Cosmos; 154/5 Designers Guild; 156/7 Osamu Murai; 158/9 Tim Street-Porter/Elizabeth Whiting & Associates; 160/161 Barbara Walz

The author and Publishers gratefully acknowledge valuable contributions and assistance from the following people and organizations:

Charles Beresford-Clark
Robyn Bowman
Jasper Conran
The Conran Shop
Inge Cordsen
Diana Corless
Garrick Davis
Richard Eagan
Denise Ford
Helena Garner
Morag Hunter
Solveig Hill
Gerard Kokt
Bob Learmonth
The London Lighting Company
Antony May
Roger Reynolds
Graeme Roberts
The Royal College of Art Library
Hilary Scarlett
Mr & Mrs Kioshi Shikita
Helen Varley
Ferry Zayadi

Artists
Jackson Day Designs/Artists Partners

Artwork/Retouching
Roy Flooks

Typesetting
Servis Filmsetting Ltd, Manchester

Printed, bound and originated in the Netherlands by Smeets Royal Offset BV, Weert